2023 CASELAW AND STATUTORY SUPPLEMENT TO

COMPUTER CRIME LAW

Fifth Edition

■ ■ ■

Orin S. Kerr

William G. Simon Professor of Law
University of California, Berkeley

AMERICAN CASEBOOK SERIES®

WEST
ACADEMIC
PUBLISHING

American Casebook Series is a trademark registered in the U.S. Patent and Trademark Office.

© 2022 LEG, Inc. d/b/a West Academic
© 2023 LEG, Inc. d/b/a West Academic
    860 Blue Gentian Road, Suite 350
    Eagan, MN 55121
    1-877-888-1330

West, West Academic Publishing, and West Academic are trademarks of West Publishing Corporation, used under license.

Printed in the United States of America

ISBN: 978-1-63659-918-2

PREFACE

This supplement serves two purposes. First, it provides caselaw updates to supplement the Fifth Edition of my casebook, COMPUTER CRIME LAW. Second, it provides the current text of the federal computer crime statutes.

The materials are current as of October 1, 2022. They are intended to be used in courses taught in the Spring 2023 and Fall 2023 semesters.

ORIN S. KERR

October 2022
Berkeley, California

TABLE OF CONTENTS

———

PART B. STATUTORY SUPPLEMENT

Introduction to the Wire-
tap Act (#22)

The consent Exception &
the Provider Exception

Stored Communications Act

TABLE OF CASES

The principal cases are in bold type.

———————

2023 CASELAW AND STATUTORY SUPPLEMENT TO
COMPUTER CRIME LAW
Fifth Edition

PART A

CASELAW SUPPLEMENT

■ ■ ■

CHAPTER 2

COMPUTER MISUSE CRIMES

■ ■ ■

C. UNAUTHORIZED ACCESS STATUTES

5. WHAT IS AUTHORIZATION? THE CASE OF NORMS-BASED RESTRICTIONS

On Page 68 through 74, replace *EF Cultural Travel BV v. Zefer Corp.* and Notes 1–2 with the following new decision and Notes:

HIQ LABS, INC. V. LINKEDIN CORP.

United States Court of Appeals for the Ninth Circuit, 2022.
31 F.4th 1180.

BERZON, CIRCUIT JUDGE.

We first issued an opinion in this case in September 2019, addressing the question whether LinkedIn, the professional networking website, could prevent a competitor, hiQ, from collecting and using information that LinkedIn users had shared on their public profiles, available for viewing by anyone with a web browser. *hiQ Labs, Inc. v. LinkedIn Corp.*, 938 F.3d 985 (9th Cir. 2019). HiQ, a data analytics company, had obtained a preliminary injunction forbidding LinkedIn from denying hiQ access to publicly available LinkedIn member profiles. At the preliminary injunction stage, we did not resolve the companies' legal dispute definitively, nor did we address all the claims and defenses they had pleaded in the district court. Instead, we focused on whether hiQ had raised serious questions on the merits of the factual and legal issues presented to us, as well as on the other requisites for preliminary relief. We concluded that hiQ had done so, and we therefore upheld the preliminary injunction.

The Supreme Court granted LinkedIn's petition for writ of certiorari, vacated the judgment, and remanded this case for further consideration in light of *Van Buren v. United States*, 141 S. Ct. 1648 (2021). We ordered supplemental briefing and held oral argument on the effect of *Van Buren* on this appeal. Having concluded that *Van Buren* reinforces our determination that hiQ has raised serious questions about whether LinkedIn may invoke the Computer Fraud and Abuse Act to preempt hiQ's

3

possibly meritorious tortious interference claim, we once again affirm the preliminary injunction.

I.

Founded in 2002, LinkedIn is a professional networking website with over 500 million members. Members post resumes and job listings and build professional "connections" with other members. LinkedIn specifically disclaims ownership of the information users post to their personal profiles: according to LinkedIn's User Agreement, members own the content and information they submit or post to LinkedIn and grant LinkedIn only a non-exclusive license to "use, copy, modify, distribute, publish, and process" that information.

LinkedIn allows its members to choose among various privacy settings. Members can specify which portions of their profile are visible to the general public (that is, to both LinkedIn members and nonmembers), and which portions are visible only to direct connections, to the member's "network" (consisting of LinkedIn members within three degrees of connectivity), or to all LinkedIn members. This case deals only with profiles made visible to the general public.

HiQ is a data analytics company founded in 2012. Using automated bots, it scrapes information that LinkedIn users have included on public LinkedIn profiles, including name, job title, work history, and skills. It then uses that information, along with a proprietary predictive algorithm, to yield "people analytics," which it sells to business clients.

In May 2017, LinkedIn sent hiQ a cease-and-desist letter, asserting that hiQ was in violation of LinkedIn's User Agreement and demanding that hiQ stop accessing and copying data from LinkedIn's server. The letter stated that if hiQ accessed LinkedIn's data in the future, it would be violating state and federal law, including the CFAA, the Digital Millennium Copyright Act, California Penal Code § 502(c), and the California common law of trespass. The letter further stated that LinkedIn had "implemented technical measures to prevent hiQ from accessing, and assisting others to access, LinkedIn's site, through systems that detect, monitor, and block scraping activity."

HiQ's response was to demand that LinkedIn recognize hiQ's right to access LinkedIn's public pages and to threaten to seek an injunction if LinkedIn refused. A week later, hiQ filed an action, seeking injunctive relief based on California law and a declaratory judgment that LinkedIn could not lawfully invoke the CFAA, the DMCA, California Penal Code § 502(c), or the common law of trespass against it. HiQ also filed a request for a temporary restraining order, which the parties subsequently agreed to convert into a motion for a preliminary injunction.

The district court granted hiQ's motion. It ordered LinkedIn to withdraw its cease-and-desist letter, to remove any existing technical barriers to hiQ's access to public profiles, and to refrain from putting in place any legal or technical measures with the effect of blocking hiQ's access to public profiles. LinkedIn timely appealed.

II.

A plaintiff seeking a preliminary injunction must establish that he is likely to succeed on the merits, that he is likely to suffer irreparable harm in the absence of preliminary relief, that the balance of equities tips in his favor, and that an injunction is in the public interest. All four elements must be satisfied.

LinkedIn argues that even if hiQ can show a likelihood of success on any of its state law causes of action, all those causes of action are preempted by the CFAA, 18 U.S.C. § 1030, which LinkedIn asserts that hiQ violated.

The pivotal CFAA question here is whether once hiQ received LinkedIn's cease-and-desist letter, any further scraping and use of LinkedIn's data was "without authorization" within the meaning of the CFAA and thus a violation of the statute. 18 U.S.C. § 1030(a)(2). If so, LinkedIn maintains, hiQ could have no legal right of access to LinkedIn's data and so could not succeed on any of its state law claims, including the tortious interference with contract claim we have held otherwise sufficient for preliminary injunction purposes.

We have held in another context that the phrase " 'without authorization' is a non-technical term that, given its plain and ordinary meaning, means accessing a protected computer without permission." *United States v. Nosal*, 844 F.3d 1024, 1028 (9th Cir. 2016) (*Nosal II*). *Nosal II* involved an employee accessing without permission an employer's private computer for which access permissions in the form of user accounts were required. *Nosal II* did not address whether access can be "without authorization" under the CFAA where, as here, prior authorization is not generally required, but a particular person—or bot—is refused access. HiQ's position is that *Nosal II* is consistent with the conclusion that where access is open to the general public, the CFAA "without authorization" concept is inapplicable. At the very least, we conclude, hiQ has raised a serious question as to this issue.

First, the wording of the statute, forbidding access without authorization, suggests a baseline in which access is not generally available and so permission is ordinarily required. "Authorization" is an affirmative notion, indicating that access is restricted to those specially recognized or admitted. *See, e.g.,* Black's Law Dictionary (11th ed. 2019) (defining "authorization" as "official permission to do something; sanction or warrant"). Where the default is free access without authorization, in ordinary parlance one would characterize selective denial of access as a ban, not as a lack of "authorization."

Second, even if this interpretation is debatable, the legislative history of the statute confirms our understanding. The CFAA was enacted to prevent intentional intrusion onto someone else's computer—specifically, computer hacking. *See United States v. Nosal,* 676 F.3d 854, 858 (9th Cir. 2012) (*Nosal I*) (citing S. Rep. No. 99–432, at 9 (1986).

The 1984 House Report on the CFAA explicitly analogized the conduct prohibited by section 1030 to forced entry: "It is noteworthy that section 1030 deals with an 'unauthorized access' concept of computer fraud rather than the mere use of a computer. Thus, the conduct prohibited is analogous to that of 'breaking and entering.'" H.R. Rep. No. 98–894, at 20 (1984); *see also id.* at 10 (describing the problem of "'hackers' who have been able to access (trespass into) both private and public computer systems"). Senator Jeremiah Denton similarly characterized the CFAA as a statute designed to prevent unlawful intrusion into otherwise inaccessible computers, observing that "the bill makes it clear that unauthorized access to a Government computer is a trespass offense, as surely as if the offender had entered a restricted Government compound without proper authorization." 132 Cong. Rec. 27639 (1986). And when considering amendments to the CFAA two years later, the House again linked computer intrusion to breaking and entering. *See* H.R. Rep. No. 99–612, at 5–6 (1986) (describing "the expanding group of electronic trespassers," who trespass "just as much as if they broke a window and crawled into a home while the occupants were away").

We therefore look to whether the conduct at issue is analogous to "breaking and entering." H.R. Rep. No. 98–894, at 20. Significantly, the version of the CFAA initially enacted in 1984 was limited to a narrow range of computers—namely, those containing national security information or financial data and those operated by or on behalf of the government. *See* Counterfeit Access Device and Computer Fraud and Abuse Act of 1984, Pub. L. No. 98–473, § 2102, 98 Stat. 2190, 2190–91. None of the computers to which the CFAA initially applied were accessible to the general public; affirmative authorization of some kind was presumptively required.

When section 1030(a)(2)(C) was added in 1996 to extend the prohibition on unauthorized access to any "protected computer," the Senate Judiciary Committee explained that the amendment was designed "to increase protection for the privacy and confidentiality of computer information." S. Rep. No. 104–357, at 7. The legislative history of section 1030 thus makes clear that the prohibition on unauthorized access is properly understood to apply only to private information—information delineated as private through use of a permission requirement of some sort. As one prominent commentator has put it, "an authentication requirement, such as a password gate, is needed to create the necessary barrier that divides open spaces from closed spaces on the Web." Orin S. Kerr, *Norms of Computer Trespass*, 116 Colum. L. Rev. 1143, 1161 (2016). Moreover, elsewhere in the statute, password fraud is cited as a means by which a computer may be accessed without authorization, see 18 U.S.C. § 1030(a)(6), bolstering the idea that authorization is only required for password-protected sites or sites that otherwise prevent the general public from viewing the information.

We therefore conclude that hiQ has raised a serious question as to whether the reference to access "without authorization" limits the scope of the statutory coverage to computers for which authorization or access permission, such as password authentication, is generally required. Put differently, the CFAA contemplates the existence of three kinds of computer systems: (1) computers for which access is open to the general public and permission is not required, (2) computers for which authorization is required and has been given, and (3) computers for which authorization is required but has not been given (or, in the case of the prohibition on exceeding authorized access, has not been given for the part of the system accessed). Public LinkedIn profiles, available to anyone with an Internet connection, fall into the first category. With regard to websites made freely accessible on the Internet, the "breaking and entering" analogue invoked so frequently during congressional consideration has no application, and the concept of "without authorization" is inapt.

The reasoning of *Van Buren* reinforces our interpretation of the CFAA, although it did not directly address the statute's "without authorization" clause. *Van Buren*'s "gates-up-or-down inquiry" is consistent with our interpretation of the CFAA as contemplating three categories of computer systems. Discussing the "without authorization" clause, *Van Buren* explained that a computer user who has authorization is one who can access a computer system, where 'access' means the act of entering a computer system itself. In other words, a user with authorization is not subject to limitations on access, whether those limitations are "code-based" or "contained in contracts or policies." *Id*. at 1659 n.8. *Van Buren* stated that the CFAA's password-trafficking provision, section 1030(a)(6), which also uses the word authorization, "contemplates a 'specific type of authorization—that is, authentication,' which turns on whether a user's credentials allow him to proceed past a computer's access gate, rather than on other, scope-based restrictions." *Id*. at 1659 n.9 (quoting Patricia L. Bellia, *A Code-Based Approach to Unauthorized Access Under the Computer Fraud and Abuse Act*, 84 Geo. Wash. L. Rev. 1442, 1470 (2016)).

Van Buren's distinction between computer users who "can or cannot access a computer system" suggests a baseline in which there are limitations on access that prevent some users from accessing the system (i.e., a "gate" exists, and can be either up or down). The Court's "gates-up-

or-down inquiry" thus applies to the latter two categories of computers we have identified: if authorization is required and has been given, the gates are up; if authorization is required and has *not* been given, the gates are down. As we have noted, however, a defining feature of public websites is that their publicly available sections lack limitations on access; instead, those sections are open to anyone with a web browser. In other words, applying the "gates" analogy to a computer hosting publicly available webpages, that computer has erected no gates to lift or lower in the first place. *Van Buren* therefore reinforces our conclusion that the concept of "without authorization" does not apply to public websites.

Additionally, neither of the cases LinkedIn principally relies upon casts doubt on our interpretation of the statute. LinkedIn first cites *Nosal II*. As we have already stated, *Nosal II* held that a former employee who used current employees' login credentials to access company computers and collect confidential information had acted "without authorization in violation of the CFAA." The computer information the defendant accessed in *Nosal II* was thus plainly one which no one could access without authorization.

So too with regard to the system at issue in *Facebook v. Power Ventures*, 844 F.3d 1058 (9th Cir. 2016), the other precedent upon which LinkedIn relies. In that case, Facebook sued Power Ventures, a social networking website that aggregated social networking information from multiple platforms, for accessing Facebook users' data and using that data to send mass messages as part of a promotional campaign. After Facebook sent a cease-and-desist letter, Power Ventures continued to circumvent IP barriers and gain access to password-protected Facebook member profiles. We held that after receiving an individualized cease-and-desist letter, Power Ventures had accessed Facebook computers "without authorization" and was therefore liable under the CFAA. But we specifically recognized that "Facebook has tried to limit and control access to its website" as to the purposes for which Power Ventures sought to use it. *Id.* at 1063. Indeed, Facebook requires its users to register with a unique username and password, and Power Ventures required that Facebook users provide their Facebook username and password to access their Facebook data on Power Ventures' platform. While Power Ventures was gathering user data that was protected by Facebook's username and password authentication system, the data hiQ was scraping was available to anyone with a web browser.

In sum, *Nosal II* and *Power Ventures* control situations in which authorization generally is required and has either never been given or has been revoked. As *Power Ventures* indicated, the two cases do not control the situation present here, in which information is presumptively open to all comers. As to the computers at issue in those cases, the authorization gate was "down."

Finally, the rule of lenity favors our narrow interpretation of the "without authorization" provision in the CFAA. The statutory prohibition on unauthorized access applies both to civil actions and to criminal prosecutions—indeed, § 1030 is primarily a criminal statute. Because we must interpret the statute consistently, whether we encounter its application in a criminal or noncriminal context, the rule of lenity applies. As we explained in *Nosal I*, we therefore favor a narrow interpretation of the CFAA's "without authorization" provision so as not to turn a criminal hacking statute into a sweeping Internet-policing mandate.

For all these reasons, it appears that the CFAA's prohibition on accessing a computer "without authorization" is violated when a person circumvents a computer's generally applicable rules regarding access permissions, such as username and password requirements, to gain access to a computer. It is likely that when a computer network generally permits public access to its data, a user's accessing that publicly available data will not constitute access without authorization under the CFAA. The data hiQ seeks to access is not owned by LinkedIn and has not been demarcated by LinkedIn as private using such an authorization system. HiQ has therefore raised serious questions about whether LinkedIn may invoke the CFAA to preempt hiQ's possibly meritorious tortious interference claim.

NOTES AND QUESTIONS

1. *The limited question in hiQ Labs.* The Ninth Circuit in hiQ Labs focuses on whether hiQ raised "serious questions" about whether it violated the CFAA. You may be wondering: Why did the court only consider this limited question? Why didn't the court simply answer whether hiQ actually did violate the CFAA? The reasons are complicated, but here is an overview.

First, note the odd way the CFAA was raised. You might have expected that LinkedIn sued hiQ for violating the CFAA. Not so: hiQ had actually sued LinkedIn. HiQ claimed that LinkedIn's efforts to block hiQ's access to LinkedIn's website violated California state law on intentional interference with contracts. HiQ had then sought and obtained a preliminary injunction stopping LinkedIn from blocking hiQ's access to LinkedIn's website. The lawfulness of hiQ's conduct under the CFAA was raised by LinkedIn only as an affirmative defense. California state law could not prohibit LinkedIn from blocking hiQ's acts, LinkedIn argued, if hiQ's acts violated the federal CFAA.

The "serious questions" test then arose under Ninth Circuit precedent on preliminary injunctions. Under that precedent, a preliminary injunction is appropriate when the plaintiff can show that the balance of hardships "tips sharply in plaintiff's favor" and the plaintiff can show at least "serious questions going to the merits" of the underlying claim. Alliance for the Wild Rockies v. Cottrell, 632 F.3d 1127, 1131–35 (9th Cir. 2011). In a part of *hiQ Labs* omitted from the excerpt above, the Ninth Circuit concluded that hiQ had shown that the balance of hardships tipped sharply in its favor. As a result, whether hiQ's effort to obtain a preliminary injunction should succeed depended on whether hiQ raised "serious questions" about the merits of its case. *Id.*

2.   *The unclear role of cease-and-desist letters.* Does the Ninth Circuit's opinion in hiQ Labs persuasively distinguish *Power Ventures* (see p. 65), the Ninth Circuit's earlier case on cease-and-desist letters and CFAA authorization? Under *hiQ Labs*, a cease-and-desist letter does not withdraw authorization to access a public website. The gate to the public website is up, and the cease-and-desist letter does not lower the gate to block access. In contrast, *Power Ventures* held that a cease-and-desist letter withdraws authorization to access a password-protected website. In the language of *Van Buren*, as applied in *hiQ Labs*, that gate was down. But does this mean a cease-and-desist letter lowers the gate in one context but not in the other? If so, why should that be?

The answer may depend on how you apply *Van Buren*'s gate framework to a password-sharing case like *Power Ventures*. Accessing a Facebook account requires a username and password. At the outset, the gate is down and accessed is blocked. If the user permits third-party access, but Facebook withdraws its permission, does the user's permission raise the gate to the third party—with Facebook's opposition then lowering it back down? Or is the user's permission insufficient to raise the gate, with the cease-and-desist letter merely emphasizing that the gate is still closed?

On page 79, add the following new Notes 6 to 9:

6.   *Using an app that secretly collects data.* If you use an app on your phone that collects data about you from your phone without your knowledge, does the app exceed authorized access to your phone in violation of the CFAA? In *Wilson v. Triller, Inc.*, ___ F.Supp.3d ___, 2022 WL 1138073 (S.D.N.Y. 2022), a class action lawsuit was brought under the CFAA against Triller, a social media app similar to TikTok. The plaintiffs, led by Wilson, argued that Triller violated the CFAA by collecting information that users did not permit it to collect. Judge Rakoff held that, assuming the factual allegations were true, such access nonetheless did not violate the CFAA:

> It is not the case that Triller collects this information by accessing parts of [Wilson's] device that she expected or understood to be "off limits" to Triller. *Van Buren*, 141 S. Ct. at 1662. Rather, Wilson merely alleges that Triller collects and then shares information about the manner in which she and other users interact through the App with Triller own servers. Thus, at most, Wilson alleges that Triller misused the information it collected about her, which is insufficient to state a claim under the CFAA.

> Wilson responds by likening the present case to *Feldman v. Comp Trading, LLC*, 2021 WL 930222 (E.D.N.Y. 2021), a case in which a court denied a motion to dismiss a CFAA claim premised on the defendant's unauthorized access to the plaintiff's data hosted on a

third-party cloud-based server. But while a plaintiff's cloud account on a third-party server may conceivably be a "protected computer" within the meaning of the statute because of the way in which cloud accounts mimic local computer storage, it does not follow that Triller improperly accessed Wilson's device when it collected information about how Wilson interacted with Triller's own servers. Thus, Wilson has not plausibly alleged that Triller exceeded its authorized access in violation of CFAA.

Id. at *4.

7.   *Who controls authorization for a shared account?* In *Sartori v. Schrodt*, 2021 WL 6060975 (11th Cir. 2021), Schrodt set up a Skype account using her family's computer. Schrodt's husband, Sartori, was the primary user of the Skype account. Years later, Schrodt logged in to the account using the username and password she had set up for it. Upon logging in, Schrodt found evidence that Sartori was engaged in extramarital affairs. Sartori later sued Schrodt under the CFAA. According to Sartori, he was the primary user of the account and therefore controlled authorization. In his view, Schrodt's use of the credentials to log in without his permission was "without authorization." The Eleventh Circuit ruled that Schrodt's access was authorized:

> One who is the creator and (as here) at least the co-owner of an online account is surely authorized to access it. Although neither the CFAA nor the SCA defines "authorization," Merriam-Webster explains that term to mean "the state of being authorized" and goes on to explain "authorize" to mean "to endorse, empower, justify, or permit by or as if by some recognized or proper authority." Who but the creator and co-owner of the Skype account—here, Schrodt—could possibly be the "proper authority"? End of story.

Id. at *3.

8.   *DOJ announces that it will not prosecute defendants for "good-faith security research."* In 2022, the Justice Department announced a new charging policy in CFAA cases. The most important provision states that DOJ will not bring prosecutions for "good-faith security research." *See* https://www.justice. gov/opa/press-release/file/1507126/download (May 19, 2022). The policy states:

> The attorney for the government should decline prosecution if available evidence shows the defendant's conduct consisted of, and the defendant intended, good-faith security research. For purposes of this policy, the attorney for the government should apply the definition of "good-faith security research" recommended by the Register of Copyrights in *Section 1201 Rulemaking: Eighth Triennial Proceeding to Determine Exemptions to the Prohibition on Circumvention*, at 258 (Oct. 2021). That is: "good faith security research" means accessing a computer solely for purposes of good-faith testing, investigation, and/or correction of a security flaw or vulnerability, where such activity is carried out in a manner designed

to avoid any harm to individuals or the public, and where the information derived from the activity is used primarily to promote the security or safety of the class of devices, machines, or online services to which the accessed computer belongs, or those who use such devices, machines, or online services. Security research not conducted in good faith—for example, for the purpose of discovering security holes in devices, machines, or services in order to extort the owners of such devices, machines, or services—might be called "research," but is not in good faith.

9.   *Breach notification laws.* Several states have state laws requiring the disclosure of computer network breaches. *See generally* Mark Verstraete & Tal Zarsky *Optimizing Breach Notification*, 2021 U. Ill. L. Rev. 803, 810–12 (2021). In March 2022, Congress enacted a new federal breach notification law, the Cyber Incident Reporting for Critical Infrastructure Act of 2022 (CIRCIA). *See* H.R. 2471 Consolidated Appropriations Act of 2022, Division Y. CIRCIA gives regulatory authority to a federal agency, the Cybersecurity and Infrastructure Security Agency (CISA), to enact federal regulations on the reporting of cyber incidents and ransom payments. As of the time this supplement is going to print, CISA has begun the process of seeking public comments for what those regulations should be. No regulations have yet been enacted.

CHAPTER 5

THE FOURTH AMENDMENT

■ ■ ■

A. THE REQUIREMENT OF GOVERNMENT ACTION

At the bottom of page 410, add the following new Note 6:

6. *State action when Internet providers have ongoing contact with law enforcement.* In *United States v. Rosenow*, 33 F.4th 529 (9th Cir. 2022), the Internet provider Yahoo received a tip that ten Yahoo users in the Philippines were using their accounts to sell CSAM. Yahoo investigated the tip and found over one hundred Yahoo accounts actively involved in child exploitation. Yahoo contacted federal law enforcement, and Yahoo officials met with government officials to report their findings. The FBI opened an investigation, and Yahoo later informed the FBI about particular users suspected of involvement based on its investigation. One such user was Rosenow. Yahoo's search of Rosenow's Messenger account indicated that he had traveled from the United States to the Philippines for purposes of child exploitation.

Yahoo's report about Rosenow led the FBI to discover Rosenow's Facebook account. When the FBI served subpoenas on Facebook for records about the account, Facebook conducted its own investigation and learned that Rosenow was engaged in child exploitation. Facebook informed law enforcement of its findings, and the FBI used Facebook's report as a basis to arrest Rosenow when he returned from the Philippines. The FBI also used the information to obtain a warrant to search Rosenow's electronic devices for CSAM. Searching those devices revealed large amounts of CSAM.

On appeal following Rosenow's conviction, the Ninth Circuit ruled that Yahoo and Facebook had remained private actors under the Fourth Amendment:

> Here, the record establishes that Yahoo and Facebook investigated Rosenow's accounts to further their own legitimate, independent motivations. As the district court found, both companies have legitimate business reasons for purging child pornography and exploitation from their platforms, and they acted in furtherance of those reasons when they investigated Rosenow. Yahoo's Director of Threat Investigations and Intelligence testified that it is "very bad for Yahoo's brand" if its services are viewed as "a haven for child pornography or child exploitation or sex trafficking." He also stated that "ridding our products and services of child abuse images is

critically important to protecting our users, our products, our brand, and our business interests."

Finally, he stated that Yahoo has a direct financial interest in keeping child pornography off its platforms because Yahoo does not want to lose advertising opportunities or be blocked from app stores. A Facebook analyst familiar with that company's internal search policies likewise explained that Facebook has a business purpose in keeping its platform safe and free from harmful content and conduct that sexually exploits children, which is why Facebook prohibits content that sexually exploits or endangers children. She testified that Facebook's policy of conducting limited review of accounts in cases indicating child exploitation is to keep its platform safe and so users will continue to use its platform.

Id. at 544–45.

Judge Graber dissented in part. Although she agreed that Facebook had remained a private actor, Judge Graber concluded that Yahoo had become a state actor when it searched Rosenow's Messenger account because its purpose was to help law enforcement. This intent was clear, Judge Graber reasoned, because Yahoo's policy was to suspend accounts only if it discovered CSAM images or video—contents that the Messenger service did not store, and that Yahoo's search of the Messenger account therefore could not reveal:

Yahoo had a legitimate reputational interest in preventing its services from being used to exploit or abuse children. But, under the specific facts of this case, that legitimate interest was dependent on—not independent from—governmental action.

It is undisputed that, during the relevant period, Yahoo did not store photographs or videos or other files shared between two users via its Messenger chat application. Indeed, any videos or images sent via the Messenger chat application were never transmitted to Yahoo servers, so there was no record of any file transfer of videos or images that would have been available for Yahoo's review. At all relevant times, Yahoo's policy allowed Yahoo to terminate a user's account on the ground of child exploitation *only* if it discovered actual images or videos of child pornography.

Despite that clear limitation, Yahoo's investigators used internal tools to review Defendant's full chat history on the Yahoo Messenger and reported many chat snippets verbatim to the government. Yahoo's investigators determined that pulling the content, reviewing it, and then filing reports to the government might be a way to get the suspected child-abuse activity to stop. When asked whether the mechanism for stopping the activity was helping to provide probable cause to federal law enforcement, Yahoo's lead investigator replied in the affirmative.

Id. at 552 (Graber, J., dissenting in part). The majority responded to Judge Graber's dissent with two arguments:

> First, it was not a foregone conclusion at the outset of Yahoo's search that it would not find any images that would permit it to close Rosenow's account without law enforcement involvement. While Yahoo did not retain images sent through its Messenger service during the relevant period, it did retain its users' Messenger profile pictures and images sent by users through its email service. Yahoo's searches included these locations where images were retained.

> Second, a private party's otherwise legitimate, independent motivation is not rendered invalid just because law enforcement assistance may further its interests.

Id. at 544–45.

B. DEFINING SEARCHES AND SEIZURES

1. SEARCHES

b) Searches of Stand-Alone Computers

On page 428, at the top, add the following new Note 13:

13. *Does unlocking a phone itself constitute a search?* When the government has seized a locked phone, agents may locate a person who claims to know the passcode that can unlock it. The agents will need a warrant to search the phone. But if agents merely enter in the alleged passcode to see if it unlocks the phone, and the phone then unlocks, does the unlocking itself constitute a search? *See United States v. Jackson*, 2021 WL 4892223 (D. Minn. 2021) (holding that "simply using a passcode to unlock Defendant's cellphone without exploring the contents of the phone does not constitute a search under the Fourth Amendment"). Should the answer depend on whether agents turn off the unlocked phone without seeing any of its contents, such as the icons that are visible on the home screen or the chosen background image?

c) Searches in the Network Context

(2) Contents of Computer Communications

On page 446, add this addendum to the existing Note 7:

The effect of terms of service on Fourth Amendment rights recently arose in two cases: Commonwealth v. Dunkins, 263 A.3d 247 (Pa. 2021), and United States v. Sporn, 2022 WL 656165 (D. Kan. 2022).

In *Dunkins*, a student at Moravian College entered a dormitory to commit a robbery inside. As he entered the building, his cell phone automatically joined the university WiFi network associated with that dormitory. Later, investigators accessed the records of which devices had logged on to the dormitory network when the crime occurred. Dunkins became a suspect when his phone was found on that list, as Dunkins did not live in that dorm. When Dunkins was charged with robbery, he argued that collecting the records of his logins violated his Fourth Amendment rights. As Note 6 on page 468 of your casebook explains, the Pennsylvania Superior Court ruled that Dunkins had no rights in the records because they were not content records.

The Pennsylvania Supreme Court reviewed the Superior Court's decision and reached the same result but for a different reason. According to the Pennsylvania Supreme Court, Dunkins had no Fourth Amendment rights because he had "abandoned any purported expectation of privacy in the WiFi connection records by consenting to the college's Computing Resources Policy." *Id.* at 253.

> By assenting to the Computing Resources Policy and logging on to the Moravian College WiFi network on his cell phone thereafter, appellant specifically agreed he "cannot and should not have any expectation of privacy with regard to any data created or stored on computers within or connected to the institution's network." Computing Resources Policy. Appellant further agreed "all Internet data composed, transmitted, or received through the institution's computer system is considered part of the institution's records and, as such, subject at any time to disclosure to institutional officials, law enforcement, or third parties."

> These acts by appellant provide clear intent to relinquish any purported expectation of privacy in the WiFi connection records. Furthermore, this abandonment by appellant was voluntary. Although appellant was required to assent to the Computing Resources Policy and other policies in the Student Handbook prior to enrolling at Moravian College, he further acquiesced to the consequences of the Computing Resources Policy upon "logging in to or otherwise connecting to the campus network." Nothing in the Computing Resources Policy required appellant to log on to Moravian's WiFi network on his cell phone and remain connected on that device at all times, but he did so voluntarily. Accordingly, we have little difficulty concluding appellant abandoned any purported expectation of privacy in the WiFi connection records and his suppression motion was properly denied. We therefore affirm the order of the Superior Court.

Id. at 255–56.

In United States v. Sporn, 2022 WL 656165 (D.Kan. 2022), Twitter received a tip that an account holder was using an account to transmit CSAM using private messages. Twitter investigated the tip, found CSAM, suspended the account, and reported the violation to the government. An investigation followed, which led to a search of the account contents Twitter had preserved.

The account holder, Sporn, later challenged the search as a violation of his Fourth Amendment rights.

The District Court ruled that Sporn had no reasonable expectation of privacy in his Twitter account, including private messages, because he had violated Twitter's terms of service:

> Twitter explicitly informs users that they are responsible for "compliance with applicable laws" in general, and specifically states that the platform has "zero tolerance" for child sexual exploitation. Twitter tells users that it "reserves the right to access and read" user information to enforce the TOS. The linked Privacy Policy informs user that "we will store and process your Direct Message communications," but notes that this processing "includes link scanning for malicious content, including the detection of spam, abuse and prohibited images."

> The linked child sexual exploitation policy of Twitter explains that any person, "whether they have a Twitter account or not," may report a potential policy violation, using a form to explain what "led you to believe the account should be reviewed." Thus, the TOS thus warns users that Twitter may scan individual communications, including direct messages for policy violations, as well as generally review an entire account if it receives a report of a potential violation of the child sexual exploitation policy.

> Defendant has pointed to no decision holding a social media user enjoys a reasonable expectation of privacy where the platform deploys a similarly robust reservation of rights by its TOS. The Court finds under the circumstances of the case and in light of Twitter's express zero tolerance policy for child sexual exploitation, once Defendant violated that policy, he lacked a reasonable expectation of privacy in the Twitter account.

Id. at *10.

Should terms of service have the power to eliminate Fourth Amendment rights, either by stating users have no privacy or by expressing conditions on privacy that users might violate? Terms of service govern almost every Internet account. Many have broad language limiting privacy rights. If those terms control, how much protection can the Fourth Amendment extend to the Internet?

On page 450, at the top, add the following new Note 9:

9. *Fourth Amendment rules for searching an image copy.* When the government seizes an electronic device, agents typically make a perfect copy of the data known as an "image." Agents will then search the image, rather than the original, in order to protect the evidentiary integrity of the original. The image is a perfect copy of the data now stored on a government-owned machine. Is the Fourth Amendment framework for searching the image the same as the

framework for searching the original? Or can the government search the image with fewer or no restrictions because it is merely data stored on a government-owned machine rather than the suspect's property?

In People v. McCavitt, 185 N.E.3d 1192 (Ill. 2021), the Illinois Supreme Court ruled that the rules for searching an image are the same as the rules for searching the original:

> The evidentiary value of data resides in the data itself, not in the medium on which it is stored. To suggest that defendant lacked an expectation of privacy in the contents of his personal computer because those contents were copied to another medium contravenes the requirement of reasonableness, which is the touchstone of any fourth amendment analysis. Imaging a computer should be regulated by the Fourth Amendment and searches of copies should be treated the same as searches of the original because computers work by copying and recopying information. Treating a digital copy as the original recognizes that the key to Fourth-Amendment reasonableness is the access to data, regardless of whether the data is copied, transferred, or otherwise manipulated.

Id. at 1206.

(3) Non-Content Account Records

On page 468, add the following addendum to Note 6:

See also Kelly v. United States, 281 A.3d 610 (D.C. 2022) (holding that subway system surveillance, in which the police were notified in real time whenever Kelly entered or left a DC Metro station by swiping his card, is not a search under *Carpenter*; it "simply provided sporadic information about Mr. Kelly's location in a public place at particular moments" and "did not permit Mr. Kelly's precise movements to be continuously monitored in real time").

C. EXCEPTIONS TO THE WARRANT REQUIREMENT

2. EXIGENT CIRCUMSTANCES

On page 506, near the bottom, add the following new Notes 4 and 5:

4.   *Exigent circumstances when a target acts suspiciously.* In United States v. Meyer, 19 F.4th 1028 (8th Cir. 2021), agents came to Meyer's home to investigate reports that he was involved in child exploitation offenses. Agents asked to speak with Meyer out in their car, and there agents confronted Meyer with his alleged ties to individuals in the Philippines who were believed to be orchestrating the illicit acts. Meyer acknowledged that he knew the individuals, and that he had communicated with them using his computers

and cell phone in his home. When agents asked Meyer for his consent to search his devices for evidence, Meyer replied that he would consent if he could first have time alone to "check email and stuff." Agents countered that this would give Meyer time to delete evidence. Meyer responded that he did not want agents to enter his house because it was "a mess" and "not in any condition to entertain people." Meyer then went back into his house.

Agents then contacted a prosecutor, who told them that exigent circumstances existed and that they should search the house without a warrant and seize the devices. The agents did so, and they later obtained warrants to search the seized computer and phone. The searches yielded the expected CSAM. The Eighth Circuit later agreed with the prosecutor that exigent circumstances existed:

> Given Meyer's insistence that he have an opportunity to be alone with his devices first, they reasonably concluded that he was hiding something. And if they were to wait to conduct the search, as he had suggested, the something that he did not want them to see would be gone. So the agents reasonably determined that it was now or never: search immediately, or forever lose their chance.

Id. at 1033.

5.   *If the government seizes phones incident to arrest, but has no plans to search them, does retaining the phones indefinitely violate the Fourth Amendment?* In most computer seizure cases, the duration of the seizure becomes relevant when the government later obtains a search warrant to search the device. If the government detained the device for too long before obtaining a warrant, the search warrant may be too late and the evidence on the phone can be suppressed. But what if the government seizes devices and won't return them, but has no plan to search them?

This issue arose in Cameron v. District of Columbia, 2022 WL 3715779 (D.D.C. 2022), a civil suit brought by individuals who had protested for police reform and racial justice following the murder of George Floyd. The police arrested more than forty demonstrators for felony rioting, and seized their phones incident to arrest. The protesters were held for up to thirty-six hours, but the government decided not to bring charges. Curiously, however, the government decided to keep the seized cell phones. Over a period of many months, the protesters requested the return of their cell phones. The government did not return the phones.

The protesters then filed suit alleging that the indefinite detention of their phones violated the Fourth Amendment. The district court disagreed. According to the district court, the proper means of seeking the return of seized property was a statutory cause of action, Federal Rule of Criminal Procedure 41 and its state equivalents. But the continued detention of property, without searching it, did not violate the Fourth Amendment:

> Every single Circuit that has either squarely ruled on or briefly considered this issue has found that the prolonged retention of

lawfully seized property does not implicate the Fourth Amendment's protection against unreasonable seizures.

> In *Denault v. Ahern*, the First Circuit held that challenges to "the government's retention of personal property after a lawful initial seizure sound in the Fifth Amendment rather than in the Fourth." 857 F.3d 76, 84 (1st Cir. 2017). The Second Circuit in *Bennett v. Dutchess County* said that "where an initial seizure of property was reasonable, the government's failure to return the items does not state a separate Fourth Amendment claim of unreasonable seizure." 832 F. App'x. 58, 60 (2d Cir. 2020). In *Fox v. Van Oosterum*, the Sixth Circuit interpreted the word "seizure" in the Fourth Amendment to protect a person's right only in initially retaining property and not any attempt to regain it thereafter. 176 F.3d 342, 349–52 (6th Cir. 1999). The court in *Fox* held that "once the act of taking the property is complete, the seizure has ended and the Fourth Amendment no longer applies."

Id. at 3.

Does it make sense that the Fourth Amendment is violated if the government waits too long to get a warrant to search seized devices, but that it can hold on to seized devices as long as it wants without violating the Fourth Amendment? Or is the point that, if the government lawfully takes property without searching it, its indefinite detention is a potential violation of the Due Process Clause or the Takings Clause rather than the Fourth Amendment? *See, e.g.,* Kelley-Lomax v. City of Chicago, 49 F.4th 1124 (7th Cir. 2022) (holding that, when the city "disposed of" plaintiff's cell phone after his arrest when he was unable to retrieve it, any remedy must come from the Due Process clause rather than the Fourth Amendment; the Fourth Amendment "is satisfied if the seizure is reasonable when it occurs" and "does not regulate disposition of the seized property").

3. CONSENT

a) Scope of Consent

On page 513, in the middle of the page, add the following new Note 3.1 before Note 4:

3.1. *More on deception rendering consent involuntary.* In Pagán-González v. Moreno, 919 F.3d 582 (1st Cir. 2019), federal agents had reason to believe that a computer at a residential address in Puerto Rico was being used to download CSAM. Ten federal agents came to the home to investigate. The agents told the residents that they needed to search because a modem in a computer at the house was "sending a signal and/or viruses to computers in Washington." Agents asked the family for consent to inspect their computers so they could fix the modem that was sending the transmissions. The agents also explained that, if they could not make the repair, they would take the faulty computer and provide a replacement at the FBI's expense.

The members of the household signed a consent form giving the FBI permission to search the computers. A search of the family computer led to the discovery of CSAM, which is what the agents were hoping to find all along. The First Circuit ruled that the FBI's deception rendered the consent invalid:

> We have little difficulty concluding that the entry and search as alleged in Pagán-González's complaint violated the Fourth Amendment. Roughly ten FBI agents appeared at appellant's door with the alarming news that computers in Washington, D.C.—the heart of the country's political and military operations—were receiving signals or viruses from a computer at appellant's location. If the report of a virus infecting technology in the nation's capital was not itself enough to convey an urgent need to address a pressing threat, the show of force by the federal agents elevated the seriousness of the situation and communicated that the problematic computer posed a substantial threat—perhaps even to the nation's security.
>
> In short, the totality of the circumstances as alleged point strongly to a situation involving an unwitting, trusting beguilement, in which Pagán-González—pressured by the urgency of the threat posed by the ruse and intimidated by the agents' en masse arrival—felt he had no choice but to allow the agents access to his home and computer.

Id. at 597–98. The court further found that the deception was so clearly unconstitutional that the facts overcame qualified immunity and rendered the officers personally liable for the Fourth Amendment violation:

> Every reasonable officer would have understood that the ruse used here, carried out in a manner that signified an emergency, would leave an individual with effectively no choice but to allow law enforcement officers inside his home so they could attempt to alleviate the grave threat. And, in turn, a reasonable officer would have known that thus denying Pagán-González a free and unconstrained choice to forgo the constitutional protection of a warrant was a violation of his Fourth Amendment rights.

Id. at 600–01.

On page 518, add the following new addendum to Note 7:

Thomson v. State, ___ S.W. 3d ___, 2022 WL 3449815 (Tex. App. 2022), contends that the law of consent searches includes an "inadvertent misnavigation" doctrine. When a party consents to a search but allows the government to do the searching, the doctrine teaches, what an officer sees in the course of "inadvertent misnavigation" is within the scope of consent. The doctrine appears to hinge on a factual finding by the trial court: What was the officer actually thinking when he clicked on a button and found evidence?

In *Thomson*, an officer suspected that Thomson might have used a second cell phone Thomson was carrying as part of criminal activity. Thomson insisted to the officer that the phone was out of service and could not be used to make calls. Thomson further claimed to the officer that he used the second phone merely as a storage device for photos related to his work as a farmer. Thomson urged the officer, Deputy Payne, to try to make a call with the phone. Deputy Payne took the phone and found he could not place a call because it lacked prepaid minutes.

Deputy Payne testified that he then tried to put the phone away by hitting the button that would lock the phone. According to Payne's testimony, however, hitting that button instead revealed CSAM. Deputy Payne testified:

> I have an iPhone and on an iPhone, there is a centrally-located button in the middle of the phone. You hit it and it sends it back to the lock screen. As I turned to go back, I hit that. Well, he didn't have an iPhone, it was something else. And a screen full of JPEGs or thumbnails popped up. It was all very young girls in sexual positions, half-dressed or undressed.

The trial court deemed Deputy Payne's testimony credible, finding as a fact he had been trying to lock the phone when he stumbled across the CSAM images. A later warrant search through the phone revealed more than 1,400 additional images of CSAM.

The Court of Appeals ruled that, in light of the trial court's factual finding, Deputy Payne had stayed within the scope of Thomson's consent:

> Accepting the trial court's factual findings and credibility determinations, we conclude that the Fourth Amendment is not implicated because no search occurred. Deputy Payne was navigating Thomson's phone with consent. Thomson could have refused access to his locked phone. He did not. He could have held his phone and ensured that only he navigated to the pertinent phone functions. He did not. By granting consent for Deputy Payne to navigate the phone, Thomson also consented to Deputy Payne's observance of anything that came within his plain view under that consent. That included the contraband images that appeared on the screen through inadvertent misnavigation. We reach this conclusion based on the trial court's credibility determination that inadvertent misnavigation led to the display of the images, not a search.

Id. at *9.

Is the "inadvertent misnavigation" doctrine sensible? Or does it create too much of an incentive for officers to lie about their state of mind, and for trial judges to credit those lies to ensure that the evidence is admitted?

5. GOVERNMENT WORKPLACE SEARCHES

On page 561, before part D., add the following new Note 4:

4. *Privacy rights in an inadvertently-created copy.* In Smith v. Pelham, 2021 WL 5863412 (11th Cir. 2021), a city employee plugged her personal iPhone into her work computer while at work. The record indicated that, unbeknownst to her, her personal phone and work computer were configured so that backup copies of her entire phone came to be made on her government workplace computer. The city employer later searched Smith's workplace computer and found backup copies of her personal phone. Searching the phone backup copies revealed nude pictures of Smith. It also revealed browsing records showing she had been searching the web on her personal phone for a different job during government work hours.

Smith eventually sued, claiming among other things that searching the backup copies of her phone violated her Fourth Amendment rights. The Eleventh Circuit disagreed. The city's workplace policy allowed the government to search workplace computers. By storing a copy of her personal files on a government-owned workplace computer, even inadvertently, Smith had placed her information in a location where it could be searched:

> The search was of her computer, not her cell phone. Unbeknownst to Smith, when she backed up her iPhone, her cell phone data was also stored on her computer. Smith's misunderstanding or inadvertence does not control the outcome. Once the computer backed up Smith's cell phone, the previously private data became accessible to her employer. It was saved on a city computer that was connected to a city network and anyone with administrative access to the network could access the cell phone backups.

Id. at *4.

D. SEARCHING AND SEIZING COMPUTERS WITH A WARRANT

1. PROBABLE CAUSE

On page 577, in the middle of the page, add the following new Note 8:

8. *If a person's digital evidence exists, is it likely to be found inside that person's home?* In United States v. Kvashuk, 29 F.4th 1077 (9th Cir. 2022), a Microsoft employee was being investigated for a massive fraud scheme involving gift cards and related tax evasion. Agents obtained a warrant to search the suspect's home. When the search revealed evidence and charges followed, the defendant argued that the warrant was invalid because officers lacked probable cause that the evidence would be in his home. Notably, the defendant, Kvashuk, agreed that the affidavit established probable cause to

believe there was evidence if his crimes somewhere. According to Kvashuk, however, there was insufficient reason to think the evidence would be located specifically at his home.

The Ninth Circuit disagreed. According to the Ninth Circuit, "the nature of cybercrime—specifically, its reliance on computers and personal electronic devices—is relevant to probable cause for searching the suspect's residence." *Id.* at 1085.

> Here, the warrant affidavit explained in detail how Kvashuk committed the suspected crimes almost entirely via digital devices. Such devices were used to access Microsoft's online store, set up and access email accounts, conduct online research in furtherance of the scheme, purchase and redeem [the gift cards], communicate with one or more tax preparers, and conduct bitcoin transactions.

> The affidavit also pointed out that many people generally keep their cell phones and other digital devices in their home and provided extensive evidence that Kvashuk did so here. For example, the affidavit noted that (1) Kvashuk was a software engineer; (2) his house had internet service; (3) the IP address assigned to his house was used in 2018 and 2019 to access his Coinbase and Gmail accounts, both of which were involved in his scheme; (4) he emailed his tax preparer in February 2019 regarding the preparation of his false 2018 return; and (5) based on the affiant's training and experience, people often keep personal, financial, and tax records in their home, including Bitcoin private keys (essentially, passwords necessary to control their Bitcoin). All of this evidence, taken together, was enough to reasonably establish a nexus between the digital devices to be seized and Kvashuk's home.

Id. at 1086.

3.   THE PHYSICAL SEARCH STAGE

On page 606, at the bottom, add the following new Note 6:

6.   *Seizing all computers when the government has probable cause that one computer was used to commit the crime.* In *Commonwealth v. Green,* 265 A.3d 541 (Pa. 2021), investigators learned that a computer with a Comcast IP address assigned to Green's home was distributing CSAM using BitTorrent. Agents obtained a warrant to search the home. The warrant listed the following items to be seized:

> Any and all computer hardware, including, but not limited to, any equipment which can collect, analyze, create, display, convert, store, conceal, or transmit electronic, magnetic, optical or similar computer impulses or data. . . . These items will be seized and then later searched for evidence relating to the possession and/or distribution of child pornography.

The agents who executed the warrant brought a mobile forensics lab with them. The lab enabled them to "preview" each digital device for images. During the preview, agents found CSAM on Green's cell phone. The phone was seized and subject to a later forensic search that discovered 100 CSAM images.

Green argued that the warrant was overbroad because it had authorized the seizure and search of every digital device in the home. The Pennsylvania Supreme Court disagreed, ruling that "there was probable cause to search and seize all digital devices in Appellant's home."

> The warrant did not request to search a particular device or even name a particular user because there was no way for investigators to obtain that information prior to a search. Based on the information available to the corporals at the time they requested the warrant, the pornography could have been shared by any user on any device using the internet in the home. There was no way to narrow this inquiry without conducting a search.

> Ultimately, given the realistic limitations of this investigation and the nature of this crime, the warrant could not have described the device sharing the contraband with any more detail than the IP address and associated physical address. There was, nevertheless, probable cause to believe that evidence of criminality would be found on a device within the home. Stated simply, the warrant described as particularly as reasonably possible the items for which there was probable cause.

Id. at 552.

Justice Wecht dissented. According to Justice Wecht, the warrant should have only authorized the search for and seizure of one computer—specifically, the one computer used to share CSAM over BitTorrent:

> With regard to the actual demonstration of probable cause to support the sweeping search that the Pennsylvania State Police (PSP) sought in this instance, the PSP noted only that it had identified a single computer that had been using BitTorrent for purposes of sharing child pornography. Despite asserting probable cause for a single device, the PSP nonetheless asked to search for "any and all" electronic devices inside the home. The vast authorization the PSP sought was not based upon any individualized suspicion of Green's potentially criminal activities, but instead upon, inter alia, the PSP's general belief that those who possess or distribute child pornography "sometimes" keep copies of the illicit contraband "in the privacy and security of their home." The PSP did not assert that specific probable cause existed to believe that Green had done so, only that some people "sometimes" do.

> Based upon the apparent probable cause as to this one device, and the generalized assertions about how offenders of this type are believed to act, the PSP was issued a warrant allowing its troopers to

seize virtually any device in Green's home capable of electronic storage and to search anywhere on those devices for evidence related to the receipt, distribution, or possession of child pornography. For all practical purposes, the PSP was permitted to enter Green's residence, seize any devices with a plug, remove them from the property, and then rummage through every digital file and any app on each device—without limitation—in the hope of discovering evidence of any kind of any wrongdoing. The result was the discovery of approximately one hundred images of child pornography on Green's smart phone.

The Majority discerns no constitutional problems with the expansive seizure and searches that occurred in this case. In my view, the Majority's decision eviscerates the particularity requirement as it applies to searches and seizures of digital devices—a problematic result in this day and age when more and more private information is being stored on our laptops and smart phones. The result enables police to conduct unbridled scavenges of digital devices that would not be permitted when performing a search in any other context.

Id. at 563–64 (Wecht, J., dissenting). If a court were to adopt Justice Wecht's view, how would the government know in advance which was the one computer used to share CSAM using BitTorrent? And if there was one computer used to share CSAM, what are the odds that there is CSAM on some other electronic storage device at the same residence?

5. EX ANTE RESTRICTIONS ON COMPUTER WARRANTS

On page 635, in the middle of the page, add the following new Note 9:

9. *The Eleventh Circuit on remedies for violations of ex ante restrictions.* In United States v. Nicholson, 24 F.4th 1341 (11th Cir. 2022), a magistrate judge imposed an ex ante restriction on a computer warrant stating that "the computer or electronic media search authorized by this warrant shall be completed within sixty (60) days of the date of this warrant." The FBI executed the warrant, seized a laptop computer, and sent the computer to a different office for a forensic examination. The forensic analyst tasked with searching the computer was unaware of the ex ante restriction. Six months passed before the seized computer was imaged and then searched. When charges were brought based on the evidence found in the computer, the defendant moved to suppress the evidence based on the failure of the FBI to follow the time limit imposed by the magistrate judge.

The Eleventh Circuit ruled that violating the ex ante condition should not lead to suppression of the evidence. First, suppression was unwarranted under the Fourth Amendment because the delay did not lead to a violation of the Fourth Amendment itself:

> Although the government did not comply with the temporal limitation in the magistrate judge's order, we cannot say that this failure rises to a Fourth Amendment violation. In contrast to the Federal Rules of Criminal Procedure, the Fourth Amendment does not specify that search warrants contain expiration dates" and contains no requirements about when the search or seizure is to occur or the duration thereof. Accordingly, when the police complete a search after the deadline in a warrant, the key constitutional question is whether the probable cause that justified the warrant went stale or dissipated because of the delay.
>
> As relevant here, the circumstances providing the probable cause to search the electronically stored images on a laptop in police custody did not dissipate or go stale over 100 days. For this reason, the probable cause that justified the initial seizure of the laptop continued to justify the belated search, and the delay between the seizure of the laptop and the search of the laptop was not constitutionally unreasonable.

Id. at 1351.

Second, suppression was not justified based on the violation of the restriction itself. Here the court borrowed from the standard used to determine when violations of analogous limits in the Federal Rules of Criminal Procedure lead to suppression:

> Instead of rising to the level of a Fourth Amendment violation, we believe the government's belated search in this case is comparable to a violation of Rule 41 of the Rules of Criminal Procedure, which contains a temporal limitation similar to the magistrate judge's addendum. We have held that noncompliance with Rule 41 requires suppression of evidence only where (1) there was 'prejudice' in the sense that the search might not have occurred or would not have been so abrasive if the rule had been followed, or (2) there is evidence of intentional and deliberate disregard of a provision in the Rule.
>
> Applying the same test here, we conclude that suppression is unwarranted. First, Nicholson does not contend that there was prejudice. The FBI seized the laptop the day after obtaining the warrant. Complying with the addendum would not have stopped the FBI from conducting a digital forensic examination of the laptop nor would it have rendered that examination any less abrasive. Second, there is no evidence of intentional or deliberate disregard for the addendum's temporal limitations. Nicholson acknowledges that the FBI employee in Birmingham who conducted the analysis was simply unaware of the existence or lapse of the sixty-day limitation. In the absence of grounds for suppression under our Rule 41 standard, we

conclude that the district court did not err in denying Nicholson's suppression motion as to images found on the laptop.

Id. at 1351–52.

CHAPTER 6

STATUTORY PRIVACY PROTECTIONS

■ ■ ■

A. THE WIRETAP ACT

1. THE BASIC STRUCTURE

On page 667, add the following addendum to Note 3:

The meaning of "contemporanous transmission" is currently being litigated in New Jersey state court in a case involving the monitoring of a Facebook account. *See* Facebook v. State, 273 A.3d 958 (N.J. Super. 2022), *motion for leave to appeal granted*, 277 A.3d 465 (N.J. 2022). In the case, state law enforcement obtained search warrants compelling Facebook to turn over the contents of two suspects' Facebook inbox every fifteen minutes for thirty days. Each warrant was a regular probable cause warrant—known under New Jersey state law as a communications data warrant, or CDW—rather than a wiretap order. Facebook objected, claiming that obtaining account contents every 15 minutes amounted to interception under the Wiretap Act and its New Jersey equivalent. According to Facebook, the state was required to obtain a wiretap order before Facebook could comply with the order.

The Superior Court, Appellate Division, initially ruled that no wiretap order was required because obtaining account contents every 15 minutes was not an interception:

> Because the officers here would have no way to catch the communications at issue in flight, before they came to rest in electronic storage on Facebook's servers, the CDWs did not authorize the "interception" of any communications at all, and did not, in that respect, implicate the federal or state [Wiretap] Acts.

Id. at 974. The Superior Court distinguished *Szymuszkiewicz*:

> The CDWs did not grant access to the contents of prospective communications on [the target's] Facebook accounts while they were either en route, or within the same second, that they were placed on Facebook's servers. Rather, police would not have access until, at earliest, fifteen minutes after any electronic communication's transmission. Though the CDWs compelled Facebook to disclose the entire stored contents of each target's Facebook account for thirty prospective days, that did not make the disclosures contemporaneous with transmission. Rather, once the communications would come to

rest on Facebook's servers, they would be in "electronic storage," and thereby subject not to the wiretap acts, but to the SCA and the provisions of [New Jersey privacy law] that mirror that statute.

Id.

Facebook then sought review of the ruling in the New Jersey Supreme Court, which agreed to review the Superior Court's decision. As of the time this supplement is going to print, the briefing before the state supreme court is ongoing and the case is still pending.

D. THE STORED COMMUNICATIONS ACT

1. THE BASIC STRUCTURE

On page 728, at the top, add the following new Note 9:

9. *Distinguishing contents and non-content records when the government seeks non-content records linked to contents.* In *Dist. of Columbia v. Meta Platforms, Inc.,* 2022 WL 805196 (D.C. Super. 2022), the District of Columbia government served a subpoena on Meta (formerly Facebook) for the identities of Facebook users that Meta had determined violated its content moderation policies for vaccine misinformation through public posts. Meta refused to comply with the subpoena. According to Meta, disclosing which users had violated its content moderation policies about vaccine misinformation would implicitly reveal contents that could not be obtained with a mere subpoena under the SCA. The Superior Court agreed with Meta:

> The logical and practical effect of revealing the identities of these users is to reveal the contents of their communications. That is because the District wants Meta to identify individual users based on the contents of their communications. The District seeks the identity only of users who Meta determined provided information about vaccines that was false, so identifying them necessarily means disclosing that they communicated information about vaccines.
>
> *Rainsy v. Facebook, Inc.,* 311 F. Supp.3d 1101, 1114–15 (N.D. Cal. 2018), supports the Court's conclusion. *Rainsy* found that disclosure of the identities of users who 'liked" a social networking page involved the contents of communications because the "like" conveyed approval of a particular message. Similarly, the inclusion of the users whose identities are sought by the District on Meta's list of violators conveys information about the content of their postings—specifically, that they provided false information about COVID-19 vaccines.
>
> According to the District, the violations are not tied to one particular message, but they are—a message about whether people should get vaccinated against COVID-19. As the District says, the specifics of the message may vary: for example, some users may encourage vaccines use, and others may discourage it; some users may talk

about side effects, and some may not; some may encourage interference with vaccine administration, and some encourage cooperation. But the essential part of the communication is the same, even if the details vary.

Id. at *4–*5.

2.   COMPELLED DISCLOSURE UNDER § 2703

On page 740, near the top, add the following new Note 12:

12.   *Applying the SCA to suspended accounts.* In Republic of the Gambia v. Facebook, Inc., 575 F.Supp.3d 8 (D.D.C. 2021), the government of The Republic of the Gambia, a small country in West Africa, sought to obtain the Facebook communications of Myanmar officials for use in a case before the International Court of Justice. The Gambia contended that the private Facebook communications of Myanmar officials would help establish Myanmar's genocide against the Rohingya people. Facebook had deleted the accounts years earlier, along with related Facebook groups, out of concern that they potentially played a role in ethnic violence against the Rohingya. Facebook had kept copies of what it deleted, however, and The Gambia sought copies of the deleted content information that Facebook had retained.

Whether The Gambia could obtain the deleted Facebook content records raised a novel question under the SCA: If a social media company deletes an account but preserves a copy of it, is the stored copy still protected by the SCA? That question turned on the ECS/RCS distinction: Is the social media company acting as an RCS, an ECS, or neither, with respect to that stored copy?

The Gambia argued that Facebook was not acting as an ECS or an RCS with respect to the stored copy, and therefore that Facebook could disclose the account contents to The Gambia without violating 18 U.S.C. § 2702. Initially, a Magistrate Judge agreed, ruling that Facebook was acting neither as an ECS nor an ECS with respect to the account contents and that the contents could therefore be disclosed to The Gambia. *See* Republic of the Gambia v. Facebook, Inc., 567 F.Supp.3d 291 (D.D.C. 2021) (Faruqui, Magistrate Judge).

Facebook then sought review of the decision from the District Court. The District Court disagreed with the Magistrate Judge, ruling that the contents were still protected by the SCA and that disclosure to The Gambia was not permitted. According to the District Court, retained messages from deleted accounts were protected under the ECS rules because they were stored "for purposes of backup protection" under 18 U.S.C. § 2510(17)(B):

> The SCA does not define "backup protection," and so the Court turns, as it must, to the plain meaning of the text. The most relevant definition of "backup" is a copy of computer data. "Backup" is also defined as a reserve or substitute. Backup, The American Heritage Dictionary of the English Language (3d ed. 1992) (published six years after SCA's passage). "Protection" is "the act of protecting," which is

defined, in turn, as "keeping from being damaged, attacked, stolen, or injured." A communication is stored "for purposes of backup protection," then, when it is a copy or reserve held to prevent it being damaged or lost.

Copies of the deleted private accounts and pages, and the communications associated with them, fall within this definition. When it deleted these pages and accounts, Facebook preserved data, including content, on the accounts and Pages it removed. Facebook stored a duplicate of these communications, among other reasons, in case it was lawfully called upon to produce them by an international body like the United Nations after their removal. Such storage was not unusual, as Facebook routinely stores removed communications in case a user petitions Facebook successfully to restore their account to the platform. These duplicates exist on the same servers, in the same place, in the same format, in exactly the same manner as they did before the accounts and pages were removed. That constitutes a "copy" or "reserve" of communications stored to prevent their loss or destruction. As a result, Facebook's storage of these communications literally falls within the statutory definition of for purposes of backup protection.

The Gambia protests that the common understanding of "backup" requires the existence of an original; in other words, if the original is deleted, the backup then becomes the primary. But dictionary definitions of "backup" require no such thing; indeed, the idea that a backup is a copy or reserve seems to contemplate the potential loss of any "original."

Id. at 13–14.

CHAPTER 7

JURISDICTION

■ ■ ■

C. INTERNATIONAL COMPUTER CRIMES

1. UNITED STATES SUBSTANTIVE LAW

On page 824, at the top, add the following new Note 8:

8. *Committing wire fraud from a foreign country.* In United States v. Elbaz, 39 F.4th 214 (4th Cir. 2022), the defendant Elbaz devised and carried out a massive fraud scheme in Israel that targeted victims worldwide. Elbaz was eventually prosecuted for wire fraud in Maryland based on three Maryland victims of the fraud. Elbaz argued that she could not be prosecuted because the wire fraud statute, 18 U.S.C. § 1343, only applied inside the United States.

The Fourth Circuit ruled that Elbaz had violated the wire fraud statute from Israel. Although the statute applied only inside the United States, the court reasoned, Elbaz had used wires inside the United States to commit the fraud and therefore violated United States law:

> We agree with Elbaz that the wire-fraud statute provides no affirmative directive that overcomes the presumption against extraterritoriality. Nowhere within the wire-fraud statute did Congress clearly indicate that it applied to foreign conduct. There is one reference to "foreign commerce," but it is not enough to rebut the presumption. Section 1343 includes a jurisdictional hook, limiting its application to wires made "in interstate or foreign commerce." 18 U.S.C. § 1343. Yet a general reference to foreign commerce in the definition of "interstate commerce" does not defeat the presumption against extraterritoriality. Rather, such language generally is intended to bring commerce between a foreign country and a state within the statute's reach. Because this jurisdictional language fails to rebut the presumption against extraterritorial application, and there are no other indications of extraterritorial application, the statute does not apply to extraterritorial conduct.
>
> Having found that wire fraud is limited to domestic conduct, we turn to step two of our inquiry. There, we must identify the wire-fraud statute's focus. The statutory focus is the object of the statute's solicitude—which can turn on the conduct, parties, or interests that it regulates or protects. And to determine the focus, we turn to the text and structure of the act, without regard for any secret concern of

members of Congress. If the conduct relevant to the statute's focus occurred in the United States, then the case involves a permissible domestic application even if other conduct occurred abroad.

The wire-fraud statute has three elements. Two are substantive: (1) the defendant devised, or intended to devise, a scheme or artifice to defraud; and (2) the defendant used a wire to transmit any signal to execute the scheme or artifice. The third element is jurisdictional: The wire must be "in interstate or foreign commerce." We can easily reject this third, jurisdictional element as the statutory focus. The substantive elements primarily define the behavior that the statute calls a violation of federal law. The substantive elements describe the harm or evil the law seeks to prevent. The jurisdictional element, by contrast, merely ties the substantive offense to one of Congress's constitutional powers. So jurisdictional elements are never the statute's focus—the conduct, parties, or interest that the statute seeks to regulate.

The focus must thus be either the scheme to defraud or the use of wire communication for executing the scheme. The statute's text and our precedent reveal that the focus of the wire-fraud statute is the use of a wire, not the scheme to defraud. The wire transmission itself is the actus reus that is punishable by federal law. Thus, the use of a wire is the essential conduct prohibited by § 1343.

Unlike the wire-transmission element, a scheme to defraud is not an essential conduct element of wire fraud. The devisal of a scheme relates only to establishing the mens rea element of the wire fraud offense. Indeed, no scheme need be devised at all. It suffices for the defendant to "intend" to devise a scheme. § 1343. So while a scheme to defraud (or at least the intention to devise a scheme) remains a necessary element, it is not the essential conduct being criminalized and thus not the focus of § 1343.

Our sister circuits that have addressed this issue agree that the focus of the wire-fraud statute is the use of a wire to execute a scheme. See, e.g., United States v. Hussain, 972 F.3d 1138, 1143–45 (9th Cir. 2020); United States v. McLellan, 959 F.3d 442, 469 (1st Cir. 2020). Joining them, we agree Elbaz's conviction must stand as a "permissible domestic application" so long as the charged wire transmissions were domestic. They were. Transmission of a message in furtherance of the scheme occurs in at least two locations: where the wire transmission at issue originated and where it was received. Here, the transmissions were received by victims in Maryland using wires in Maryland. So Elbaz's convictions are all permissible domestic applications of the wire-fraud statute.

Id. at 222–24.

4. MUTUAL LEGAL ASSISTANCE

c) Cross-Border Data Requests Under the Cloud Act of 2018

On page 869, replace Note 2 with the following new Note 2:

2. *Australia is set to become the second "qualifying foreign government" by the end of 2022.* In December 2021, the Australian Minister for Home Affairs and the United States Attorney General signed a US-Australia CLOUD Act Agreement. The agreement followed the passage by the Australian Parliament of the *Telecommunications Legislation Amendment (International Production Orders) Act 2021*, which was needed to make Australia compliant with the CLOUD Act. It is expected that the US-Australia CLOUD Act Agreement will go into effect by the end of 2022. When this occurs, Australia will become the second "qualifying foreign government" under the CLOUD Act. *See generally* Australia-US CLOUD Act Agreement, https://www.homeaffairs.gov.au/about-us/our-portfolios/national-security/lawful-access-telecommunications/australia-united-states-cloud-act-agreement.

PART B

STATUTORY SUPPLEMENT

■ ■ ■

18 U.S.C. § 641. Public Money, Property or Records

Whoever embezzles, steals, purloins, or knowingly converts to his use or the use of another, or without authority, sells, conveys or disposes of any record, voucher, money, or thing of value of the United States or of any department or agency thereof, or any property made or being made under contract for the United States or any department or agency thereof; or

Whoever receives, conceals, or retains the same with intent to convert it to his use or gain, knowing it to have been embezzled, stolen, purloined or converted—

Shall be fined under this title or imprisoned not more than ten years, or both; but if the value of such property in the aggregate, combining amounts from all the counts for which the defendant is convicted in a single case, does not exceed the sum of $1,000, he shall be fined under this title or imprisoned not more than one year, or both.

The word "value" means face, par, or market value, or cost price, either wholesale or retail, whichever is greater.

18 U.S.C. § 875. Interstate Communications

(a) Whoever transmits in interstate or foreign commerce any communication containing any demand or request for a ransom or reward for the release of any kidnapped person, shall be fined under this title or imprisoned not more than twenty years, or both.

(b) Whoever, with intent to extort from any person, firm, association, or corporation, any money or other thing of value, transmits in interstate or foreign commerce any communication containing any threat to kidnap any person or any threat to injure the person of another, shall be fined under this title or imprisoned not more than twenty years, or both.

(c) Whoever transmits in interstate or foreign commerce any communication containing any threat to kidnap any person or any threat to injure the person of another, shall be fined under this title or imprisoned not more than five years, or both.

(d) Whoever, with intent to extort from any person, firm, association, or corporation, any money or other thing of value, transmits in interstate or foreign commerce any communication containing any threat to injure the property or reputation of the addressee or of another or the reputation of a deceased person or any threat to accuse the addressee or any other person of a crime, shall be fined under this title or imprisoned not more than two years, or both.

18 U.S.C. § 1028. FRAUD AND RELATED ACTIVITY IN CONNECTION WITH IDENTIFICATION DOCUMENTS, AUTHENTICATION FEATURES, AND INFORMATION

(a) Whoever, in a circumstance described in subsection (c) of this section—

(1) knowingly and without lawful authority produces an identification document, authentication feature, or a false identification document;

(2) knowingly transfers an identification document, authentication feature, or a false identification document knowing that such document or feature was stolen or produced without lawful authority;

(3) knowingly possesses with intent to use unlawfully or transfer unlawfully five or more identification documents (other than those issued lawfully for the use of the possessor), authentication features, or false identification documents;

(4) knowingly possesses an identification document (other than one issued lawfully for the use of the possessor), authentication feature, or a false identification document, with the intent such document or feature be used to defraud the United States;

(5) knowingly produces, transfers, or possesses a document-making implement or authentication feature with the intent such document-making implement or authentication feature will be used in the production of a false identification document or another document-making implement or authentication feature which will be so used;

(6) knowingly possesses an identification document or authentication feature that is or appears to be an identification document or authentication feature of the United States or a sponsoring entity of an event designated as a special event of national significance which is stolen or produced without lawful authority knowing that such document or feature was stolen or produced without such authority;

(7) knowingly transfers, possesses, or uses, without lawful authority, a means of identification of another person with the intent to commit, or to aid or abet, or in connection with, any unlawful activity that constitutes a violation of Federal law, or that constitutes a felony under any applicable State or local law; or

(8) knowingly traffics in false or actual authentication features for use in false identification documents, document-making implements, or means of identification; shall be punished * * *.

* * *

(c) The circumstance referred to in subsection (a) of this section is that—

(1) the identification document, authentication feature, or false identification document is or appears to be issued by or under the authority of the United States or a sponsoring entity of an event designated as a special event of national significance or the document-making implement is designed or suited for making such an identification document, authentication feature, or false identification document;

(2) the offense is an offense under subsection (a)(4) of this section; or

(3) either—

(A) the production, transfer, possession, or use prohibited by this section is in or affects interstate or foreign commerce, including the transfer of a document by electronic means; or

(B) the means of identification, identification document, false identification document, or document-making implement is transported in the mail in the course of the production, transfer, possession, or use prohibited by this section.

(d) In this section and section 1028A—

(1) the term "authentication feature" means any hologram, watermark, certification, symbol, code, image, sequence of numbers or letters, or other feature that either individually or in combination with another feature is used by the issuing authority on an identification document, document-making implement, or means of identification to determine if the document is counterfeit, altered, or otherwise falsified;

(2) the term "document-making implement" means any implement, impression, template, computer file, computer disc, electronic device, or computer hardware or software, that is specifically configured or primarily used for making an identification document, a false identification document, or another document-making implement;

(3) the term "identification document" means a document made or issued by or under the authority of the United States Government, a State, political subdivision of a State, a sponsoring entity of an event designated as a special event of national significance, a foreign government, political subdivision of a foreign government, an international governmental or an international quasi-governmental organization which, when completed with information concerning a particular individual, is of a type intended or commonly accepted for the purpose of identification of individuals;

(4) the term "false identification document" means a document of a type intended or commonly accepted for the purposes of identification of individuals that—

(A) is not issued by or under the authority of a governmental entity or was issued under the authority of a governmental entity but was subsequently altered for purposes of deceit; and

(B) appears to be issued by or under the authority of the United States Government, a State, a political subdivision of a State, a sponsoring entity of an event designated by the President as a special event of national significance, a foreign government, a political subdivision of a foreign government, or an international governmental or quasi-governmental organization;

(5) the term "false authentication feature" means an authentication feature that—

(A) is genuine in origin, but, without the authorization of the issuing authority, has been tampered with or altered for purposes of deceit;

(B) is genuine, but has been distributed, or is intended for distribution, without the authorization of the issuing authority and not in connection with a lawfully made identification document, document-making implement, or means of identification to which such authentication feature is intended to be affixed or embedded by the respective issuing authority; or

(C) appears to be genuine, but is not;

(6) the term "issuing authority"—

(A) means any governmental entity or agency that is authorized to issue identification documents, means of identification, or authentication features; and

(B) includes the United States Government, a State, a political subdivision of a State, a sponsoring entity of an event designated by the President as a special event of national significance, a foreign government, a political subdivision of a foreign government, or an international government or quasi-governmental organization;

(7) the term "means of identification" means any name or number that may be used, alone or in conjunction with any other information, to identify a specific individual, including any—

(A) name, social security number, date of birth, official State or government issued driver's license or identification number, alien registration number, government passport number, employer or taxpayer identification number;

(B) unique biometric data, such as fingerprint, voice print, retina or iris image, or other unique physical representation;

(C) unique electronic identification number, address, or routing code; or

(D) telecommunication identifying information or access device (as defined in section 1029(e));

(8) the term "personal identification card" means an identification document issued by a State or local government solely for the purpose of identification;

(9) the term "produce" includes alter, authenticate, or assemble;

(10) the term "transfer" includes selecting an identification document, false identification document, or document-making implement and placing or directing the placement of such identification document, false identification document, or document-making implement on an online location where it is available to others;

(11) the term "State" includes any State of the United States, the District of Columbia, the Commonwealth of Puerto Rico, and any other commonwealth, possession, or territory of the United States; and

(12) the term "traffic" means—

(A) to transport, transfer, or otherwise dispose of, to another, as consideration for anything of value; or

(B) to make or obtain control of with intent to so transport, transfer, or otherwise dispose of.

(e) This section does not prohibit any lawfully authorized investigative, protective, or intelligence activity of a law enforcement agency of the United States, a State, or a political subdivision of a State, or of an intelligence agency of the United States, or any activity authorized under chapter 224 of this title.

(f) Attempt and conspiracy.—Any person who attempts or conspires to commit any offense under this section shall be subject to the same penalties as those prescribed for the offense, the commission of which was the object of the attempt or conspiracy.

18 U.S.C. § 1028A. AGGRAVATED IDENTITY THEFT

(a) Offenses.

(1) In general. Whoever, during and in relation to any felony violation enumerated in subsection (c), knowingly transfers, possesses, or uses, without lawful authority, a means of identification of another person shall, in addition to the punishment provided for such felony, be sentenced to a term of imprisonment of 2 years.

(2) Terrorism offense. Whoever, during and in relation to any felony violation enumerated in section 2332b(g)(5)(B), knowingly transfers, possesses, or uses, without lawful authority, a means of identification of another person or a false identification document shall, in addition to the punishment provided for such felony, be sentenced to a term of imprisonment of 5 years.

* * *

(c) Definition. For purposes of this section, the term "felony violation enumerated in subsection (c)" means any offense that is a felony violation of—

(1) section 641 (relating to theft of public money, property, or records), section 656 (relating to theft, embezzlement, or misapplication by bank officer or employee), or section 664 (relating to theft from employee benefit plans);

(2) section 911 (relating to false personation of citizenship);

(3) section 922(a)(6) (relating to false statements in connection with the acquisition of a firearm);

(4) any provision contained in this chapter (relating to fraud and false statements), other than this section or section 1028(a)(7);

(5) any provision contained in chapter 63 (relating to mail, bank, and wire fraud);

(6) any provision contained in chapter 69 (relating to nationality and citizenship);

(7) any provision contained in chapter 75 (relating to passports and visas);

(8) section 523 of the Gramm-Leach-Bliley Act (15 U.S.C. 6823) (relating to obtaining customer information by false pretenses);

(9) section 243 or 266 of the Immigration and Nationality Act (8 U.S.C. 1253 and 1306) (relating to willfully failing to leave the United States after deportation and creating a counterfeit alien registration card);

(10) any provision contained in chapter 8 of title II of the Immigration and Nationality Act (8 U.S.C. 1321 et seq.) (relating to various immigration offenses); or

(11) section 208, 811, 1107(b), 1128B(a), or 1632 of the Social Security Act (42 U.S.C. 408, 1011, 1307(b), 1320a–7b(a), and 1383a) (relating to false statements relating to programs under the Act).

18 U.S.C. § 1029. FRAUD AND RELATED ACTIVITY IN CONNECTION WITH ACCESS DEVICES

(a) Whoever—

(1) knowingly and with intent to defraud produces, uses, or traffics in one or more counterfeit access devices;

(2) knowingly and with intent to defraud traffics in or uses one or more unauthorized access devices during any one-year period, and by such conduct obtains anything of value aggregating $1,000 or more during that period;

(3) knowingly and with intent to defraud possesses fifteen or more devices which are counterfeit or unauthorized access devices;

(4) knowingly, and with intent to defraud, produces, traffics in, has control or custody of, or possesses device-making equipment;

(5) knowingly and with intent to defraud effects transactions, with 1 or more access devices issued to another person or persons, to receive payment or any other thing of value during any 1-year period the aggregate value of which is equal to or greater than $1,000;

(6) without the authorization of the issuer of the access device, knowingly and with intent to defraud solicits a person for the purpose of—

(A) offering an access device; or

(B) selling information regarding or an application to obtain an access device;

(7) knowingly and with intent to defraud uses, produces, traffics in, has control or custody of, or possesses a telecommunications instrument that has been modified or altered to obtain unauthorized use of telecommunications services;

(8) knowingly and with intent to defraud uses, produces, traffics in, has control or custody of, or possesses a scanning receiver;

(9) knowingly uses, produces, traffics in, has control or custody of, or possesses hardware or software, knowing it has been configured to insert or modify telecommunication identifying information associated with or contained in a telecommunications instrument so

that such instrument may be used to obtain telecommunications service without authorization; or

(10) without the authorization of the credit card system member or its agent, knowingly and with intent to defraud causes or arranges for another person to present to the member or its agent, for payment, 1 or more evidences or records of transactions made by an access device;

shall, if the offense affects interstate or foreign commerce, be punished as provided in subsection (c) of this section.

(b)(1)   Whoever attempts to commit an offense under subsection (a) of this section shall be subject to the same penalties as those prescribed for the offense attempted.

(2)   Whoever is a party to a conspiracy of two or more persons to commit an offense under subsection (a) of this section, if any of the parties engages in any conduct in furtherance of such offense, shall be fined an amount not greater than the amount provided as the maximum fine for such offense under subsection (c) of this section or imprisoned not longer than one-half the period provided as the maximum imprisonment for such offense under subsection (c) of this section, or both.

* * *

(e) As used in this section—

(1) the term "access device" means any card, plate, code, account number, electronic serial number, mobile identification number, personal identification number, or other telecommunications service, equipment, or instrument identifier, or other means of account access that can be used, alone or in conjunction with another access device, to obtain money, goods, services, or any other thing of value, or that can be used to initiate a transfer of funds (other than a transfer originated solely by paper instrument);

(2) the term "counterfeit access device" means any access device that is counterfeit, fictitious, altered, or forged, or an identifiable component of an access device or a counterfeit access device;

(3) the term "unauthorized access device" means any access device that is lost, stolen, expired, revoked, canceled, or obtained with intent to defraud;

(4) the term "produce" includes design, alter, authenticate, duplicate, or assemble;

(5) the term "traffic" means transfer, or otherwise dispose of, to another, or obtain control of with intent to transfer or dispose of;

(6) the term "device-making equipment" means any equipment, mechanism, or impression designed or primarily used for making an access device or a counterfeit access device;

(7) The term "credit card system member" means a financial institution or other entity that is a member of a credit card system, including an entity, whether affiliated with or identical to the credit card issuer, that is the sole member of a credit card system;

(8) the term "scanning receiver" means a device or apparatus that can be used to intercept a wire or electronic communication in violation of chapter 119 or to intercept an electronic serial number, mobile identification number, or other identifier of any telecommunications service, equipment, or instrument;

(9) the term "telecommunications service" has the meaning given such term in section 3 of title I of the Communications Act of 1934 (47 U.S.C. § 153);

(10) the term "facilities-based carrier" means an entity that owns communications transmission facilities, is responsible for the operation and maintenance of those facilities, and holds an operating license issued by the Federal Communications Commission under the authority of title III of the Communications Act of 1934; and

(11) the term "telecommunication identifying information" means electronic serial number or any other number or signal that identifies a specific telecommunications instrument or account, or a specific communication transmitted from a telecommunications instrument.

(f) This section does not prohibit any lawfully authorized investigative, protective, or intelligence activity of a law enforcement agency of the United States, a State, or a political subdivision of a State, or of an intelligence agency of the United States, or any activity authorized under chapter 224 of this title. For purposes of this subsection, the term "State" includes a State of the United States, the District of Columbia, and any commonwealth, territory, or possession of the United States.

(g)(1) It is not a violation of subsection (a)(9) for an officer, employee, or agent of, or a person engaged in business with, a facilities-based carrier, to engage in conduct (other than trafficking) otherwise prohibited by that subsection for the purpose of protecting the property or legal rights of that carrier, unless such conduct is for the purpose of obtaining telecommunications service provided by another facilities-based carrier without the authorization of such carrier.

(2) In a prosecution for a violation of subsection (a)(9), (other than a violation consisting of producing or trafficking) it is an affirmative defense (which the defendant must establish by a preponderance of the evidence) that the conduct charged was engaged in for research or development in connection with a lawful purpose.

(h) Any person who, outside the jurisdiction of the United States, engages in any act that, if committed within the jurisdiction of the United States, would constitute an offense under subsection (a) or (b) of this section, shall be subject to the fines, penalties, imprisonment, and forfeiture provided in this title if—

> **(1)** the offense involves an access device issued, owned, managed, or controlled by a financial institution, account issuer, credit card system member, or other entity within the jurisdiction of the United States; and

> **(2)** the person transports, delivers, conveys, transfers to or through, or otherwise stores, secrets, or holds within the jurisdiction of the United States, any article used to assist in the commission of the offense or the proceeds of such offense or property derived therefrom.

18 U.S.C. § 1030.　Fraud and Related Activity in Connection with Computers

(a) Whoever—

> **(1)** having knowingly accessed a computer without authorization or exceeding authorized access, and by means of such conduct having obtained information that has been determined by the United States Government pursuant to an Executive order or statute to require protection against unauthorized disclosure for reasons of national defense or foreign relations, or any restricted data, as defined in paragraph y. of section 11 of the Atomic Energy Act of 1954, with reason to believe that such information so obtained could be used to the injury of the United States, or to the advantage of any foreign nation willfully communicates, delivers, transmits, or causes to be communicated, delivered, or transmitted, or attempts to communicate, deliver, transmit or cause to be communicated, delivered, or transmitted the same to any person not entitled to receive it, or willfully retains the same and fails to deliver it to the officer or employee of the United States entitled to receive it;

> **(2)** intentionally accesses a computer without authorization or exceeds authorized access, and thereby obtains—

>> **(A)** information contained in a financial record of a financial institution, or of a card issuer as defined in section 1602(n) of title 15, or contained in a file of a consumer reporting agency on a consumer, as such terms are defined in the Fair Credit Reporting Act (15 U.S.C. 1681 et seq.);

(B) information from any department or agency of the United States; or

(C) information from any protected computer;

(3) intentionally, without authorization to access any nonpublic computer of a department or agency of the United States, accesses such a computer of that department or agency that is exclusively for the use of the Government of the United States or, in the case of a computer not exclusively for such use, is used by or for the Government of the United States and such conduct affects that use by or for the Government of the United States;

(4) knowingly and with intent to defraud, accesses a protected computer without authorization, or exceeds authorized access, and by means of such conduct furthers the intended fraud and obtains anything of value, unless the object of the fraud and the thing obtained consists only of the use of the computer and the value of such use is not more than $5,000 in any 1-year period;

(5)(A) knowingly causes the transmission of a program, information, code, or command, and as a result of such conduct, intentionally causes damage without authorization, to a protected computer;

(B) intentionally accesses a protected computer without authorization, and as a result of such conduct, recklessly causes damage; or

(C) intentionally accesses a protected computer without authorization, and as a result of such conduct, causes damage and loss.

(6) knowingly and with intent to defraud traffics (as defined in section 1029) in any password or similar information through which a computer may be accessed without authorization, if—

(A) such trafficking affects interstate or foreign commerce; or

(B) such computer is used by or for the Government of the United States;

(7) with intent to extort from any person any money or other thing of value, transmits in interstate or foreign commerce any communication containing any—

(A) threat to cause damage to a protected computer;

(B) threat to obtain information from a protected computer without authorization or in excess of authorization or to impair the confidentiality of information obtained from a protected computer without authorization or by exceeding authorized access; or

(C) demand or request for money or other thing of value in relation to damage to a protected computer, where such damage was caused to facilitate the extortion;

shall be punished as provided in subsection (c) of this section.

(b) Whoever conspires to commit or attempts to commit an offense under subsection (a) of this section shall be punished as provided in subsection (c) of this section.

(c) The punishment for an offense under subsection (a) or (b) of this section is—

(1)(A) a fine under this title or imprisonment for not more than ten years, or both, in the case of an offense under subsection (a)(1) of this section which does not occur after a conviction for another offense under this section, or an attempt to commit an offense punishable under this subparagraph; and

(B) a fine under this title or imprisonment for not more than twenty years, or both, in the case of an offense under subsection (a)(1) of this section which occurs after a conviction for another offense under this section, or an attempt to commit an offense punishable under this subparagraph;

(2)(A) except as provided in subparagraph (B), a fine under this title or imprisonment for not more than one year, or both, in the case of an offense under subsection (a)(2), (a)(3), or (a)(6) of this section which does not occur after a conviction for another offense under this section, or an attempt to commit an offense punishable under this subparagraph;

(B) a fine under this title or imprisonment for not more than 5 years, or both, in the case of an offense under subsection (a)(2), or an attempt to commit an offense punishable under this subparagraph, if—

(i) the offense was committed for purposes of commercial advantage or private financial gain;

(ii) the offense was committed in furtherance of any criminal or tortious act in violation of the Constitution or laws of the United States or of any State; or

(iii) the value of the information obtained exceeds $5,000; and

(C) a fine under this title or imprisonment for not more than ten years, or both, in the case of an offense under subsection (a)(2), (a)(3) or (a)(6) of this section which occurs after a conviction for another offense under this section, or an attempt to commit an offense punishable under this subparagraph;

(3)(A)   a fine under this title or imprisonment for not more than five years, or both, in the case of an offense under subsection (a)(4) or (a)(7) of this section which does not occur after a conviction for another offense under this section, or an attempt to commit an offense punishable under this subparagraph; and

(B) a fine under this title or imprisonment for not more than ten years, or both, in the case of an offense under subsection (a)(4) or (a)(7) of this section which occurs after a conviction for another offense under this section, or an attempt to commit an offense punishable under this subparagraph;

(4)(A)   except as provided in subparagraphs (E) and (F), a fine under this title, imprisonment for not more than 5 years, or both, in the case of—

(i)   an offense under subsection (a)(5)(B), which does not occur after a conviction for another offense under this section, if the offense caused (or, in the case of an attempted offense, would, if completed, have caused)—

(I)   loss to 1 or more persons during any 1-year period (and, for purposes of an investigation, prosecution, or other proceeding brought by the United States only, loss resulting from a related course of conduct affecting 1 or more other protected computers) aggregating at least $5,000 in value;

(II)   the modification or impairment, or potential modification or impairment, of the medical examination, diagnosis, treatment, or care of 1 or more individuals;

(III)   physical injury to any person;

(IV)   a threat to public health or safety;

(V)   damage affecting a computer used by or for an entity of the United States Government in furtherance of the administration of justice, national defense, or national security; or

(VI) damage affecting 10 or more protected computers during any 1-year period; or

(ii) an attempt to commit an offense punishable under this subparagraph;

(B) except as provided in subparagraphs (E) and (F), a fine under this title, imprisonment for not more than 10 years, or both, in the case of—

(i) an offense under subsection (a)(5)(A), which does not occur after a conviction for another offense under this section, if the offense caused (or, in the case of an attempted offense, would, if completed, have caused) a harm provided in subclauses (I) through (VI) of subparagraph (A)(i); or

(ii) an attempt to commit an offense punishable under this subparagraph;

(C) except as provided in subparagraphs (E) and (F), a fine under this title, imprisonment for not more than 20 years, or both, in the case of—

(i) an offense or an attempt to commit an offense under subparagraphs (A) or (B) of subsection (a)(5) that occurs after a conviction for another offense under this section; or

(ii) an attempt to commit an offense punishable under this subparagraph;

(D) a fine under this title, imprisonment for not more than 10 years, or both, in the case of—

(i) an offense or an attempt to commit an offense under subsection (a)(5)(C) that occurs after a conviction for another offense under this section; or

(ii) an attempt to commit an offense punishable under this subparagraph;

(E) if the offender attempts to cause or knowingly or recklessly causes serious bodily injury from conduct in violation of subsection (a)(5)(A), a fine under this title, imprisonment for not more than 20 years, or both;

(F) if the offender attempts to cause or knowingly or recklessly causes death from conduct in violation of subsection (a)(5)(A), a fine under this title, imprisonment for any term of years or for life, or both; or

(G) a fine under this title, imprisonment for not more than 1 year, or both, for—

(i) any other offense under subsection (a)(5); or

(ii) an attempt to commit an offense punishable under this subparagraph.

(d)(1) The United States Secret Service shall, in addition to any other agency having such authority, have the authority to investigate offenses under this section.

(2) The Federal Bureau of Investigation shall have primary authority to investigate offenses under subsection (a)(1) for any cases involving espionage, foreign counterintelligence, information protected against unauthorized disclosure for reasons of national defense or foreign relations, or Restricted Data (as that term is defined in section 11y of the Atomic Energy Act of 1954 (42 U.S.C. 2014(y)), except for offenses affecting the duties of the United States Secret Service pursuant to section 3056(a) of this title.

(3) Such authority shall be exercised in accordance with an agreement which shall be entered into by the Secretary of the Treasury and the Attorney General.

(e) As used in this section—

(1) the term "computer" means an electronic, magnetic, optical, electrochemical, or other high speed data processing device performing logical, arithmetic, or storage functions, and includes any data storage facility or communications facility directly related to or operating in conjunction with such device, but such term does not include an automated typewriter or typesetter, a portable hand held calculator, or other similar device;

(2) the term "protected computer" means a computer—

(A) exclusively for the use of a financial institution or the United States Government, or, in the case of a computer not exclusively for such use, used by or for a financial institution or the United States Government and the conduct constituting the offense affects that use by or for the financial institution or the Government;

(B) which is used in or affecting interstate or foreign commerce or communication, including a computer located outside the United States that is used in a manner that affects interstate or foreign commerce or communication of the United States; or

(C) that—

(i) is part of a voting system; and

(ii)(I) is used for the management, support, or administration of a Federal election; or

(II) has moved in or otherwise affects interstate or foreign commerce;

(3) the term "State" includes the District of Columbia, the Commonwealth of Puerto Rico, and any other commonwealth, possession or territory of the United States;

(4) the term "financial institution" means—

(A) an institution, with deposits insured by the Federal Deposit Insurance Corporation;

(B) the Federal Reserve or a member of the Federal Reserve including any Federal Reserve Bank;

(C) a credit union with accounts insured by the National Credit Union Administration;

(D) a member of the Federal home loan bank system and any home loan bank;

(E) any institution of the Farm Credit System under the Farm Credit Act of 1971;

(F) a broker-dealer registered with the Securities and Exchange Commission pursuant to section 15 of the Securities Exchange Act of 1934;

(G) the Securities Investor Protection Corporation;

(H) a branch or agency of a foreign bank (as such terms are defined in paragraphs (1) and (3) of section 1(b) of the International Banking Act of 1978); and

(I) an organization operating under section 25 or section 25(a) of the Federal Reserve Act;

(5) the term "financial record" means information derived from any record held by a financial institution pertaining to a customer's relationship with the financial institution;

(6) the term "exceeds authorized access" means to access a computer with authorization and to use such access to obtain or alter information in the computer that the accesser is not entitled so to obtain or alter;

(7) the term "department of the United States" means the legislative or judicial branch of the Government or one of the executive departments enumerated in section 101 of title 5;

(8) the term "damage" means any impairment to the integrity or availability of data, a program, a system, or information;

(9) the term "government entity" includes the Government of the United States, any State or political subdivision of the United States, any foreign country, and any state, province, municipality, or other political subdivision of a foreign country;

(10) the term "conviction" shall include a conviction under the law of any State for a crime punishable by imprisonment for more than 1 year, an element of which is unauthorized access, or exceeding authorized access, to a computer;

(11) the term "loss" means any reasonable cost to any victim, including the cost of responding to an offense, conducting a damage assessment, and restoring the data, program, system, or information to its condition prior to the offense, and any revenue lost, cost incurred, or other consequential damages incurred because of interruption of service;

(12) the term "person" means any individual, firm, corporation, educational institution, financial institution, governmental entity, or legal or other entity;

(13) the term "Federal election" means any election (as defined in section 301(1) of the Federal Election Campaign Act of 1971 (52 U.S.C. 30101(1))) for Federal office (as defined in section 301(3) of the Federal Election Campaign Act of 1971 (52 U.S.C. 30101(3))); and

(14) the term "voting system" has the meaning given the term in section 301(b) of the Help America Vote Act of 2002 (52 U.S.C. 21081(b)).

(f) This section does not prohibit any lawfully authorized investigative, protective, or intelligence activity of a law enforcement agency of the United States, a State, or a political subdivision of a State, or of an intelligence agency of the United States.

(g) Any person who suffers damage or loss by reason of a violation of this section may maintain a civil action against the violator to obtain compensatory damages and injunctive relief or other equitable relief. A civil action for a violation of this section may be brought only if the conduct involves 1 of the factors set forth in subclauses (I), (II), (III), (IV), or (V) of subsection (c)(4)(A)(i). Damages for a violation involving only conduct described in subsection (c)(4)(A)(i)(I) are limited to economic damages. No action may be brought under this subsection unless such action is begun within 2 years of the date of the act complained of or the date of the discovery of the damage. No action may be brought under this subsection for the negligent design or manufacture of computer hardware, computer software, or firmware.

(h) The Attorney General and the Secretary of the Treasury shall report to the Congress annually, during the first 3 years following the date of the enactment of this subsection, concerning investigations and prosecutions under subsection (a)(5).

(i)(1) The court, in imposing sentence on any person convicted of a violation of this section, or convicted of conspiracy to violate this section, shall order, in addition to any other sentence imposed and irrespective of any provision of State law, that such person forfeit to the United States—

   (A) such person's interest in any personal property that was used or intended to be used to commit or to facilitate the commission of such violation; and

   (B) any property, real or personal, constituting or derived from, any proceeds that such person obtained, directly or indirectly, as a result of such violation.

   (2) The criminal forfeiture of property under this subsection, any seizure and disposition thereof, and any judicial proceeding in relation thereto, shall be governed by the provisions of section 413 of the Comprehensive Drug Abuse Prevention and Control Act of 1970 (21 U.S.C. 853), except subsection (d) of that section.

(j) For purposes of subsection (i), the following shall be subject to forfeiture to the United States and no property right shall exist in them:

   (1) Any personal property used or intended to be used to commit or to facilitate the commission of any violation of this section, or a conspiracy to violate this section.

   (2) Any property, real or personal, which constitutes or is derived from proceeds traceable to any violation of this section, or a conspiracy to violate this section.

18 U.S.C. § 1084. TRANSMISSION OF WAGERING INFORMATION; PENALTIES

(a) Whoever being engaged in the business of betting or wagering knowingly uses a wire communication facility for the transmission in interstate or foreign commerce of bets or wagers or information assisting in the placing of bets or wagers on any sporting event or contest, or for the transmission of a wire communication which entitles the recipient to receive money or credit as a result of bets or wagers, or for information assisting in the placing of bets or wagers, shall be fined under this title or imprisoned not more than two years, or both.

(b) Nothing in this section shall be construed to prevent the transmission in interstate or foreign commerce of information for use in news reporting of sporting events or contests, or for the transmission of information assisting in the placing of bets or wagers on a sporting event or contest from a State or foreign country where betting on that sporting event or contest is legal into a State or foreign country in which such betting is legal.

(c) Nothing contained in this section shall create immunity from criminal prosecution under any laws of any State.

(d) When any common carrier, subject to the jurisdiction of the Federal Communications Commission, is notified in writing by a Federal, State, or local law enforcement agency, acting within its jurisdiction, that any facility furnished by it is being used or will be used for the purpose of transmitting or receiving gambling information in interstate or foreign commerce in violation of Federal, State or local law, it shall discontinue or refuse, the leasing, furnishing, or maintaining of such facility, after reasonable notice to the subscriber, but no damages, penalty or forfeiture, civil or criminal, shall be found against any common carrier for any act done in compliance with any notice received from a law enforcement agency. Nothing in this section shall be deemed to prejudice the right of any person affected thereby to secure an appropriate determination, as otherwise provided by law, in a Federal court or in a State or local tribunal or agency, that such facility should not be discontinued or removed, or should be restored.

(e) As used in this section, the term "State" means a State of the United States, the District of Columbia, the Commonwealth of Puerto Rico, or a commonwealth, territory or possession of the United States.

18 U.S.C. § 1343. FRAUD BY WIRE, RADIO, OR TELEVISION

Whoever, having devised or intending to devise any scheme or artifice to defraud, or for obtaining money or property by means of false or fraudulent pretenses, representations, or promises, transmits or causes to be transmitted by means of wire, radio, or television communication in interstate or foreign commerce, any writings, signs, signals, pictures, or sounds for the purpose of executing such scheme or artifice, shall be fined under this title or imprisoned not more than 20 years, or both. If the violation occurs in relation to, or involving any benefit authorized, transported, transmitted, transferred, disbursed, or paid in connection with, a presidentially declared major disaster or emergency (as those terms are defined in section 102 of the Robert T. Stafford Disaster Relief and Emergency Assistance Act (42 U.S.C. 5122)), or affects a financial institution, such person shall be fined not more than $1,000,000 or imprisoned not more than 30 years, or both.

18 U.S.C. § 1462. IMPORTATION OR TRANSPORTATION OF OBSCENE MATTERS

Whoever brings into the United States, or any place subject to the jurisdiction thereof, or knowingly uses any express company or other common carrier or interactive computer service (as defined in section 230(e)(2) of the Communications Act of 1934), for carriage in interstate or foreign commerce—

(a) any obscene, lewd, lascivious, or filthy book, pamphlet, picture, motion-picture film, paper, letter, writing, print, or other matter of indecent character; or

(b) any obscene, lewd, lascivious, or filthy phonograph recording, electrical transcription, or other article or thing capable of producing sound; or

(c) any drug, medicine, article, or thing designed, adapted, or intended for producing abortion, or for any indecent or immoral use; or any written or printed card, letter, circular, book, pamphlet, advertisement, or notice of any kind giving information, directly or indirectly, where, how, or of whom, or by what means any of such mentioned articles, matters, or things may be obtained or made; or

Whoever knowingly takes or receives, from such express company or other common carrier or interactive computer service (as defined in section 230(e)(2) of the Communications Act of 1934) any matter or thing the carriage or importation of which is herein made unlawful—

Shall be fined under this title or imprisoned not more than five years, or both, for the first such offense and shall be fined under this title or imprisoned not more than ten years, or both, for each such offense thereafter.

18 U.S.C. § 1465. PRODUCTION AND TRANSPORTATION OF OBSCENE MATTERS FOR SALE OR DISTRIBUTION

Whoever knowingly produces with the intent to transport, distribute, or transmit in interstate or foreign commerce, or whoever knowingly transports or travels in, or uses a facility or means of, interstate or foreign commerce or an interactive computer service (as defined in section 230(e)(2) of the Communications Act of 1934) in or affecting such commerce, for the purpose of sale or distribution of any obscene, lewd, lascivious, or filthy book, pamphlet, picture, film, paper, letter, writing, print, silhouette, drawing, figure, image, cast, phonograph recording, electrical transcription or other article capable of producing sound or any other matter of indecent or immoral character, shall be fined under this title or imprisoned not more than five years, or both.

The transportation as aforesaid of two or more copies of any publication or two or more of any article of the character described above, or a combined total of five such publications and articles, shall create a presumption that such publications or articles are intended for sale or distribution, but such presumption shall be rebuttable.

18 U.S.C. § 1831. ECONOMIC ESPIONAGE

(a) In general.—Whoever, intending or knowing that the offense will benefit any foreign government, foreign instrumentality, or foreign agent, knowingly—

(1) steals, or without authorization appropriates, takes, carries away, or conceals, or by fraud, artifice, or deception obtains a trade secret;

(2) without authorization copies, duplicates, sketches, draws, photographs, downloads, uploads, alters, destroys, photocopies, replicates, transmits, delivers, sends, mails, communicates, or conveys a trade secret;

(3) receives, buys, or possesses a trade secret, knowing the same to have been stolen or appropriated, obtained, or converted without authorization;

(4) attempts to commit any offense described in any of paragraphs (1) through (3); or

(5) conspires with one or more other persons to commit any offense described in any of paragraphs (1) through (3), and one or more of such persons do any act to effect the object of the conspiracy,

shall, except as provided in subsection (b), be fined not more than $500,000 or imprisoned not more than 15 years, or both.

(b) Organizations.—Any organization that commits any offense described in subsection (a) shall be fined not more than $10,000,000.

18 U.S.C. § 1832. THEFT OF TRADE SECRETS

(a) Whoever, with intent to convert a trade secret, that is related to a product or service used in or intended for use in interstate or foreign commerce, to the economic benefit of anyone other than the owner thereof, and intending or knowing that the offense will, injure any owner of that trade secret, knowingly—

(1) steals, or without authorization appropriates, takes, carries away, or conceals, or by fraud, artifice, or deception obtains such information;

(2) without authorization copies, duplicates, sketches, draws, photographs, downloads, uploads, alters, destroys, photocopies, replicates, transmits, delivers, sends, mails, communicates, or conveys such information;

(3) receives, buys, or possesses such information, knowing the same to have been stolen or appropriated, obtained, or converted without authorization;

(4) attempts to commit any offense described in paragraphs (1) through (3); or

(5) conspires with one or more other persons to commit any offense described in paragraphs (1) through (3), and one or more of such persons do any act to effect the object of the conspiracy, shall, except as provided in subsection (b), be fined under this title or imprisoned not more than 10 years, or both.

(b) Any organization that commits any offense described in subsection (a) shall be fined not more than the greater of $5,000,000 or 3 times the value of the stolen trade secret to the organization, including expenses for research and design and other costs of reproducing the trade secret that the organization has thereby avoided.

18 U.S.C. § 1839. DEFINITIONS

As used in this chapter—

(1) the term "foreign instrumentality" means any agency, bureau, ministry, component, institution, association, or any legal, commercial, or business organization, corporation, firm, or entity that is substantially owned, controlled, sponsored, commanded, managed, or dominated by a foreign government;

(2) the term "foreign agent" means any officer, employee, proxy, servant, delegate, or representative of a foreign government;

(3) the term "trade secret" means all forms and types of financial, business, scientific, technical, economic, or engineering information, including patterns, plans, compilations, program devices, formulas, designs, prototypes, methods, techniques, processes, procedures, programs, or codes, whether tangible or intangible, and whether or how stored, compiled, or memorialized physically, electronically, graphically, photographically, or in writing if—

(A) the owner thereof has taken reasonable measures to keep such information secret; and

(B) the information derives independent economic value, actual or potential, from not being generally known to, and not being readily ascertainable through proper means by, the public; and

(4) the term "owner", with respect to a trade secret, means the person or entity in whom or in which rightful legal or equitable title to, or license in, the trade secret is reposed.

18 U.S.C. § 2251. SEXUAL EXPLOITATION OF CHILDREN

(a) Any person who employs, uses, persuades, induces, entices, or coerces any minor to engage in, or who has a minor assist any other person to engage in, or who transports any minor in or affecting interstate or foreign commerce, or in any Territory or Possession of the United States, with the intent that such minor engage in, any sexually explicit conduct for the purpose of producing any visual depiction of such conduct or for the purpose of transmitting a live visual depiction of such conduct, shall be punished as provided under subsection (e), if such person knows or has reason to know that such visual depiction will be transported or transmitted using any means or facility of interstate or foreign commerce or in or affecting interstate or foreign commerce or mailed, if that visual depiction was produced or transmitted using materials that have been mailed, shipped, or transported in or affecting interstate or foreign commerce by any means, including by computer, or if such visual depiction has actually been transported or transmitted using any means or facility of interstate or foreign commerce or in or affecting interstate or foreign commerce or mailed.

(b) Any parent, legal guardian, or person having custody or control of a minor who knowingly permits such minor to engage in, or to assist any other person to engage in, sexually explicit conduct for the purpose of producing any visual depiction of such conduct or for the purpose of transmitting a live visual depiction of such conduct shall be punished as provided under subsection (e) of this section, if such parent, legal guardian, or person knows or has reason to know that such visual depiction will be transported or transmitted using any means or facility of interstate or foreign commerce or in or affecting interstate or foreign commerce or mailed, if that visual depiction was produced or transmitted using materials that have been mailed, shipped, or transported in or affecting interstate or foreign commerce by any means, including by computer, or if such visual depiction has actually been transported or transmitted using any means or facility of interstate or foreign commerce or in or affecting interstate or foreign commerce or mailed.

(c)(1) Any person who, in a circumstance described in paragraph (2), employs, uses, persuades, induces, entices, or coerces any minor to engage in, or who has a minor assist any other person to engage in, any sexually explicit conduct outside of the United States, its territories or possessions, for the purpose of producing any visual depiction of such conduct, shall be punished as provided under subsection (e).

(2) The circumstance referred to in paragraph (1) is that—

(A) the person intends such visual depiction to be transported to the United States, its territories or possessions, by any means, including by using any means or facility of interstate or foreign commerce or mail; or

(B) the person transports such visual depiction to the United States, its territories or possessions, by any means, including by using any means or facility of interstate or foreign commerce or mail.

(d)(1) Any person who, in a circumstance described in paragraph (2), knowingly makes, prints, or publishes, or causes to be made, printed, or published, any notice or advertisement seeking or offering—

(A) to receive, exchange, buy, produce, display, distribute, or reproduce, any visual depiction, if the production of such visual depiction involves the use of a minor engaging in sexually explicit conduct and such visual depiction is of such conduct; or

(B) participation in any act of sexually explicit conduct by or with any minor for the purpose of producing a visual depiction of such conduct:

shall be punished as provided under subsection (e).

(2) The circumstance referred to in paragraph (1) is that—

(A) such person knows or has reason to know that such notice or advertisement will be transported using any means or facility of interstate or foreign commerce or in or affecting interstate or foreign commerce by any means including by computer or mailed; or

(B) such notice or advertisement is transported using any means or facility of interstate or foreign commerce or in or affecting interstate or foreign commerce by any means including by computer or mailed.

(e) Any individual who violates, or attempts or conspires to violate, this section shall be fined under this title and imprisoned not less than 15 years nor more than 30 years, but if such person has one prior conviction under this chapter, section 1591, chapter 71, chapter 109A, or chapter 117, or under section 920 of title 10 (article 120 of the Uniform Code of Military Justice), or under the laws of any State relating to aggravated sexual abuse, sexual abuse, abusive sexual contact involving a minor or ward, or sex trafficking of children, or the production, possession, receipt, mailing, sale, distribution, shipment, or transportation of child pornography, such person shall be fined under this title and imprisoned for not less than 25 years nor more than 50 years, but if such person has 2 or more prior convictions under this chapter, chapter 71, chapter 109A, or chapter 117, or under section 920 of title 10 (article 120 of the Uniform Code of Military Justice), or under the laws of any State relating to the sexual exploitation of children, such person shall be fined under this title and imprisoned not less than 35 years nor more than life. Any organization that violates, or attempts or conspires to violate, this section shall be fined under this title. Whoever, in the course of an offense under this section, engages in conduct that results in the death of a person, shall be punished by death or imprisoned for not less than 30 years or for life.

18 U.S.C. § 2252. CERTAIN ACTIVITIES RELATING TO MATERIAL INVOLVING THE SEXUAL EXPLOITATION OF MINORS

(a) Any person who—

(1) knowingly transports or ships using any means or facility of interstate or foreign commerce or in or affecting interstate or foreign commerce by any means including by computer or mails, any visual depiction, if—

   (A) the producing of such visual depiction involves the use of a minor engaging in sexually explicit conduct; and

   (B) such visual depiction is of such conduct;

(2) knowingly receives, or distributes, any visual depiction using any means or facility of interstate or foreign commerce or that has been mailed, or has been shipped or transported in or affecting interstate or foreign commerce, or which contains materials which have been mailed or so shipped or transported, by any means including by computer, or knowingly reproduces any visual depiction for distribution using any means or facility of interstate or foreign commerce or in or affecting interstate or foreign commerce or through the mails, if—

   (A) the producing of such visual depiction involves the use of a minor engaging in sexually explicit conduct; and

   (B) such visual depiction is of such conduct;

(3) either—

   (A) in the special maritime and territorial jurisdiction of the United States, or on any land or building owned by, leased to, or otherwise used by or under the control of the Government of the United States, or in the Indian country as defined in section 1151 of this title, knowingly sells or possesses with intent to sell any visual depiction; or

   (B) knowingly sells or possesses with intent to sell any visual depiction that has been mailed, shipped, or transported using any means or facility of interstate or foreign commerce, or has been shipped or transported in or affecting interstate or foreign commerce, or which was produced using materials which have been mailed or so shipped or transported using any means or facility of interstate or foreign commerce, including by computer, if—

      (i) the producing of such visual depiction involves the use of a minor engaging in sexually explicit conduct; and

      (ii) such visual depiction is of such conduct; or

(4) either—

   (A) in the special maritime and territorial jurisdiction of the United States, or on any land or building owned by, leased to, or otherwise used by or under the control of the Government of the United States, or in the Indian country as defined in section 1151 of this title, knowingly possesses, or knowingly accesses with intent to view, 1 or more books, magazines, periodicals, films, video tapes, or other matter which contain any visual depiction; or

(B) knowingly possesses, or knowingly accesses with intent to view, 1 or more books, magazines, periodicals, films, video tapes, or other matter which contain any visual depiction that has been mailed, or has been shipped or transported using any means or facility of interstate or foreign commerce or in or affecting interstate or foreign commerce, or which was produced using materials which have been mailed or so shipped or transported, by any means including by computer, if—

(i) the producing of such visual depiction involves the use of a minor engaging in sexually explicit conduct; and

(ii) such visual depiction is of such conduct;

shall be punished as provided in subsection (b) of this section.

(b)(1) Whoever violates, or attempts or conspires to violate, paragraph (1), (2), or (3) of subsection (a) shall be fined under this title and imprisoned not less than 5 years and not more than 20 years, but if such person has a prior conviction under this chapter, section 1591, chapter 71, chapter 109A, chapter 117, or under section 920 of title 10 (article 120 of the Uniform Code of Military Justice), or under the laws of any State relating to aggravated sexual abuse, sexual abuse, or abusive sexual conduct involving a minor or ward, or the production, possession, receipt, mailing, sale, distribution, shipment, or transportation of child pornography, or sex trafficking of children, such person shall be fined under this title and imprisoned for not less than 15 years nor more than 40 years.

(2) Whoever violates, or attempts or conspires to violate, paragraph (4) of subsection (a) shall be fined under this title or imprisoned not more than 10 years, or both, but if such person has a prior conviction under this chapter, chapter 71, chapter 109A, or chapter 117, or under section 920 of Title 10 (article 120 of the Uniform Code of Military Justice), or under the laws of any State relating to aggravated sexual abuse, sexual abuse, or abusive sexual conduct involving a minor or ward, or the production, possession, receipt, mailing, sale, distribution, shipment, or transportation of child pornography, such person shall be fined under this title and imprisoned for not less than 10 years nor more than 20 years.

(c) Affirmative defense.—It shall be an affirmative defense to a charge of violating paragraph (4) of subsection (a) that the defendant—

(1) possessed less than three matters containing any visual depiction proscribed by that paragraph; and

(2) promptly and in good faith, and without retaining or allowing any person, other than a law enforcement agency, to access any visual depiction or copy thereof—

(A) took reasonable steps to destroy each such visual depiction; or

(B) reported the matter to a law enforcement agency and afforded that agency access to each such visual depiction.

18 U.S.C. § 2252A. CERTAIN ACTIVITIES RELATING TO MATERIAL CONSTITUTING OR CONTAINING CHILD PORNOGRAPHY

(a) Any person who—

(1) knowingly mails, or transports or ships using any means or facility of interstate or foreign commerce or in or affecting interstate or foreign commerce by any means, including by computer, any child pornography;

(2) knowingly receives or distributes—

(A) any child pornography using any means or facility of interstate or foreign commerce or that has been mailed, or has been shipped or transported in or affecting interstate or foreign commerce by any means, including by computer; or

(B) any material that contains child pornography using any means or facility of interstate or foreign commerce or that has been mailed, or has been shipped or transported in or affecting interstate or foreign commerce by any means, including by computer;

(3) knowingly—

(A) reproduces any child pornography for distribution through the mails, or using any means or facility of interstate or foreign commerce or in or affecting interstate or foreign commerce by any means, including by computer; or

(B) advertises, promotes, presents, distributes, or solicits through the mails, or using any means or facility of interstate or foreign commerce or in or affecting interstate or foreign commerce by any means, including by computer, any material or purported material in a manner that reflects the belief, or that is intended to cause another to believe, that the material or purported material is, or contains—

(i) an obscene visual depiction of a minor engaging in sexually explicit conduct; or

(ii) a visual depiction of an actual minor engaging in sexually explicit conduct;

(4) either—

(A) in the special maritime and territorial jurisdiction of the United States, or on any land or building owned by, leased to, or otherwise used by or under the control of the United States Government, or in the Indian country (as defined in section 1151), knowingly sells or possesses with the intent to sell any child pornography; or

(B) knowingly sells or possesses with the intent to sell any child pornography that has been mailed, or shipped or transported using any means or facility of interstate or foreign commerce or in or affecting interstate or foreign commerce by any means, including by computer, or that was produced using materials that have been mailed, or shipped or transported in or affecting interstate or foreign commerce by any means, including by computer;

(5) either—

(A) in the special maritime and territorial jurisdiction of the United States, or on any land or building owned by, leased to, or otherwise used by or under the control of the United States Government, or in the Indian country (as defined in section 1151), knowingly possesses, or knowingly accesses with intent to view, any book, magazine, periodical, film, videotape, computer disk, or any other material that contains an image of child pornography; or

(B) knowingly possesses, or knowingly accesses with intent to view, any book, magazine, periodical, film, videotape, computer disk, or any other material that contains an image of child pornography that has been mailed, or shipped or transported using any means or facility of interstate or foreign commerce or in or affecting interstate or foreign commerce by any means, including by computer, or that was produced using materials that have been mailed, or shipped or transported in or affecting interstate or foreign commerce by any means, including by computer;

(6) knowingly distributes, offers, sends, or provides to a minor any visual depiction, including any photograph, film, video, picture, or computer generated image or picture, whether made or produced by

electronic, mechanical, or other means, where such visual depiction is, or appears to be, of a minor engaging in sexually explicit conduct—

(A) that has been mailed, shipped, or transported using any means or facility of interstate or foreign commerce or in or affecting interstate or foreign commerce by any means, including by computer;

(B) that was produced using materials that have been mailed, shipped, or transported in or affecting interstate or foreign commerce by any means, including by computer; or

(C) which distribution, offer, sending, or provision is accomplished using the mails or any means or facility of interstate or foreign commerce,

for purposes of inducing or persuading a minor to participate in any activity that is illegal; or

(7) knowingly produces with intent to distribute, or distributes, by any means, including a computer, in or affecting interstate or foreign commerce, child pornography that is an adapted or modified depiction of an identifiable minor.

shall be punished as provided in subsection (b).

(b)(1) Whoever violates, or attempts or conspires to violate, paragraph (1), (2), (3), (4), or (6) of subsection (a) shall be fined under this title and imprisoned not less than 5 years and not more than 20 years, but, if such person has a prior conviction under this chapter, section 1591, chapter 71, chapter 109A, or chapter 117, or under section 920 of title 10 (article 120 of the Uniform Code of Military Justice), or under the laws of any State relating to aggravated sexual abuse, sexual abuse, or abusive sexual conduct involving a minor or ward, or the production, possession, receipt, mailing, sale, distribution, shipment, or transportation of child pornography, or sex trafficking of children, such person shall be fined under this title and imprisoned for not less than 15 years nor more than 40 years.

(2) Whoever violates, or attempts or conspires to violate, subsection (a)(5) shall be fined under this title or imprisoned not more than 10 years, or both, but, if any image of child pornography involved in the offense involved a prepubescent minor or a minor who had not attained 12 years of age, such person shall be fined under this title and imprisoned for not more than 20 years, or if such person has a prior conviction under this chapter, chapter 71, chapter 109A, or chapter 117, or under section 920 of title 10 (article 120 of the Uniform Code of Military Justice), or under the laws of any State relating to aggravated sexual abuse, sexual abuse, or abusive sexual conduct involving a minor or ward, or the production, possession, receipt, mailing, sale, distribution, shipment, or transportation of child pornography, such person shall be fined under this title and imprisoned for not less than 10 years nor more than 20 years.

(3) Whoever violates, or attempts or conspires to violate, subsection (a)(7) shall be fined under this title or imprisoned not more than 15 years, or both.

(c) It shall be an affirmative defense to a charge of violating paragraph (1), (2), (3)(A), (4), or (5) of subsection (a) that—

(1)(A)   the alleged child pornography was produced using an actual person or persons engaging in sexually explicit conduct; and

(B) each such person was an adult at the time the material was produced; or

(2) the alleged child pornography was not produced using any actual minor or minors.

No affirmative defense under subsection (c)(2) shall be available in any prosecution that involves child pornography as described in section 2256(8)(C). A defendant may not assert an affirmative defense to a charge of violating paragraph (1), (2), (3)(A), (4), or (5) of subsection (a) unless, within the time provided for filing pretrial motions or at such time prior to trial as the judge may direct, but in no event later than 14 days before the commencement of the trial, the defendant provides the court and the United States with notice of the intent to assert such defense and the substance of any expert or other specialized testimony or evidence upon which the defendant intends to rely. If the defendant fails to comply with this subsection, the court shall, absent a finding of extraordinary circumstances that prevented timely compliance, prohibit the defendant from asserting such defense to a charge of violating paragraph (1), (2), (3)(A), (4), or (5) of subsection (a) or presenting any evidence for which the defendant has failed to provide proper and timely notice.

(d) Affirmative defense. It shall be an affirmative defense to a charge of violating subsection (a)(5) that the defendant—

(1) possessed less than three images of child pornography; and

(2) promptly and in good faith, and without retaining or allowing any person, other than a law enforcement agency, to access any image or copy thereof—

(A) took reasonable steps to destroy each such image; or

(B) reported the matter to a law enforcement agency and afforded that agency access to each such image.

(e) Admissibility of evidence. On motion of the government, in any prosecution under this chapter or section 1466A, except for good cause shown, the name, address, social security number, or other nonphysical identifying information, other than the age or approximate age, of any minor who is depicted in any child pornography shall not be admissible and may be redacted from any otherwise admissible evidence, and the jury shall be instructed, upon request of the United States, that it can draw no inference from the absence of such evidence in deciding whether the child pornography depicts an actual minor.

(f) Civil remedies.—

(1) In general. Any person aggrieved by reason of the conduct prohibited under subsection (a) or (b) or section 1466A may commence a civil action for the relief set forth in paragraph (2).

(2) Relief. In any action commenced in accordance with paragraph (1), the court may award appropriate relief, including—

(A) temporary, preliminary, or permanent injunctive relief;

(B) compensatory and punitive damages; and

(C) the costs of the civil action and reasonable fees for attorneys and expert witnesses.

(g) Child exploitation enterprises.—

(1) Whoever engages in a child exploitation enterprise shall be fined under this title and imprisoned for any term of years not less than 20 or for life.

(2) A person engages in a child exploitation enterprise for the purposes of this section if the person violates section 1591, section 1201 if the victim is a minor, or chapter 109A (involving a minor victim), 110 (except for sections 2257 and 2257A), or 117 (involving a minor victim), as a part of a series of felony violations constituting three or more separate incidents and involving more than one victim, and commits those offenses in concert with three or more other persons.

18 U.S.C. § 2256. DEFINITIONS FOR CHAPTER

For the purposes of this chapter, the term—

(1) "minor" means any person under the age of eighteen years;

(2)(A) Except as provided in subparagraph (B), "sexually explicit conduct" means actual or simulated—

(i) sexual intercourse, including genital-genital, oral-genital, anal-genital, or oral-anal, whether between persons of the same or opposite sex;

(ii) bestiality;

(iii) masturbation;

(iv) sadistic or masochistic abuse; or

(v) lascivious exhibition of the anus, genitals, or pubic area of any person;

(B) For purposes of subsection 8(B) of this section, "sexually explicit conduct" means—

(i) graphic sexual intercourse, including genital-genital, oral-genital, anal-genital, or oral-anal, whether between persons of the same or opposite sex, or lascivious simulated sexual intercourse where the genitals, breast, or pubic area of any person is exhibited;

(ii) graphic or lascivious simulated;

(I) bestiality;

(II) masturbation; or

(III) sadistic or masochistic abuse; or

(iii) graphic or simulated lascivious exhibition of the anus, genitals, or pubic area of any person;

(3) "producing" means producing, directing, manufacturing, issuing, publishing, or advertising;

(4) "organization" means a person other than an individual;

(5) "visual depiction" includes undeveloped film and videotape, data stored on computer disk or by electronic means which is capable of conversion into a visual image, and data which is capable of conversion into a visual image that has been transmitted by any means, whether or not stored in a permanent format;

(6) "computer" has the meaning given that term in section 1030 of this title;

(7) "custody or control" includes temporary supervision over or responsibility for a minor whether legally or illegally obtained;

(8) "child pornography" means any visual depiction, including any photograph, film, video, picture, or computer or computer-generated image or picture, whether made or produced by electronic, mechanical, or other means, of sexually explicit conduct, where—

(A) the production of such visual depiction involves the use of a minor engaging in sexually explicit conduct;

(B) such visual depiction is a digital image, computer image, or computer-generated image that is, or is indistinguishable from, that of a minor engaging in sexually explicit conduct; or

(C) such visual depiction has been created, adapted, or modified to appear that an identifiable minor is engaging in sexually explicit conduct.

(9) "identifiable minor"—

(A) means a person—

(i)(I)   who was a minor at the time the visual depiction was created, adapted, or modified; or

(II) whose image as a minor was used in creating, adapting, or modifying the visual depiction; and

(ii) who is recognizable as an actual person by the person's face, likeness, or other distinguishing characteristic, such as a unique birthmark or other recognizable feature; and

(B) shall not be construed to require proof of the actual identity of the identifiable minor.

(10) "graphic", when used with respect to a depiction of sexually explicit conduct, means that a viewer can observe any part of the genitals or pubic area of any depicted person or animal during any part of the time that the sexually explicit conduct is being depicted; and

(11) the term "indistinguishable" used with respect to a depiction, means virtually indistinguishable, in that the depiction is such that an ordinary person viewing the depiction would conclude that the depiction is of an actual minor engaged in sexually explicit conduct. This definition does not apply to depictions that are drawings, cartoons, sculptures, or paintings depicting minors or adults.

18 U.S.C. § 2258A. REPORTING REQUIREMENTS OF PROVIDERS

(a) Duty to report.—

(1) In general.—

(A) Duty.—In order to reduce the proliferation of online child sexual exploitation and to prevent the online sexual exploitation of children, a provider—

(i) shall, as soon as reasonably possible after obtaining actual knowledge of any facts or circumstances described in paragraph (2)(A), take the actions described in subparagraph (B); and

(ii) may, after obtaining actual knowledge of any facts or circumstances described in paragraph (2)(B), take the actions described in subparagraph (B).

(B) Actions described.—The actions described in this subparagraph are—

(i) providing to the CyberTipline of NCMEC, or any successor to the CyberTipline operated by NCMEC, the mailing address, telephone number, facsimile number, electronic mailing address of, and individual point of contact for, such provider; and (ii) making a report of such facts or circumstances to the CyberTipline, or any successor to the CyberTipline operated by NCMEC.

(2) Facts or circumstances.—

(A) Apparent violations.—The facts or circumstances described in this subparagraph are any facts or circumstances from which there is an apparent violation of section 2251, 2251A, 2252, 2252A, 2252B, or 2260 that involves child pornography.

(B) Imminent violations.—The facts or circumstances described in this subparagraph are any facts or circumstances which indicate a violation of any of the sections described in subparagraph (A) involving child pornography may be planned or imminent.

(b) Contents of report.—In an effort to prevent the future sexual victimization of children, and to the extent the information is within the custody or control of a provider, the facts and circumstances included in each report under subsection (a)(1) may, at the sole discretion of the provider, include the following information:

(1) Information about the involved individual.—Information relating to the identity of any individual who appears to have violated or plans to violate a Federal law described in subsection (a)(2), which may, to the extent reasonably practicable, include the electronic mail address, Internet Protocol address, uniform resource locator, payment information (excluding personally identifiable information), or any other identifying information, including self-reported identifying information.

(2) Historical reference.—Information relating to when and how a customer or subscriber of a provider uploaded, transmitted, or received content relating to the report or when and how content relating to the report was reported to, or discovered by the provider, including a date and time stamp and time zone.

(3) Geographic location information.—Information relating to the geographic location of the involved individual or website, which may include the Internet Protocol address or verified address, or, if not reasonably available, at least one form of geographic identifying information, including area code or zip code, provided by the customer or subscriber, or stored or obtained by the provider.

(4) Visual depictions of apparent child pornography.—Any visual depiction of apparent child pornography or other content relating to the incident such report is regarding.

(5) Complete communication.—The complete communication containing any visual depiction of apparent child pornography or other content, including—

>   **(A)** any data or information regarding the transmission of the communication; and

>   **(B)** any visual depictions, data, or other digital files contained in, or attached to, the communication.

(c) Forwarding of report to law enforcement.—Pursuant to its clearinghouse role as a private, nonprofit organization, and at the conclusion of its review in furtherance of its nonprofit mission, NCMEC shall make available each report made under subsection (a)(1) to one or more of the following law enforcement agencies:

(1) Any Federal law enforcement agency that is involved in the investigation of child sexual exploitation, kidnapping, or enticement crimes.

(2) Any State or local law enforcement agency that is involved in the investigation of child sexual exploitation.

(3) A foreign law enforcement agency designated by the Attorney General under subsection (d)(3) or a foreign law enforcement agency that has an established relationship with the Federal Bureau of Investigation, Immigration and Customs Enforcement, or INTERPOL, and is involved in the investigation of child sexual exploitation, kidnapping, or enticement crimes.

(d) Attorney General responsibilities.—

(1) In general.—The Attorney General shall enforce this section.

(2) Designation of Federal agencies.—The Attorney General may designate a Federal law enforcement agency or agencies to which a report shall be forwarded under subsection (c)(1).

(3) Designation of foreign agencies.—The Attorney General may—

>   **(A)** in consultation with the Secretary of State, designate foreign law enforcement agencies to which a report may be forwarded under subsection (c)(3);

>   **(B)** establish the conditions under which such a report may be forwarded to such agencies; and

(C) develop a process for foreign law enforcement agencies to request assistance from Federal law enforcement agencies in obtaining evidence related to a report referred under subsection (c)(3).

(4) **Reporting designated foreign agencies.**—The Attorney General may maintain and make available to the Department of State, NCMEC, providers, the Committee on the Judiciary of the Senate, and the Committee on the Judiciary of the House of Representatives a list of the foreign law enforcement agencies designated under paragraph (3).

(5) **Notification to providers.**—

(A) **In general.**—NCMEC may notify a provider of the information described in subparagraph (B), if—

(i) a provider notifies NCMEC that the provider is making a report under this section as the result of a request by a foreign law enforcement agency; and

(ii) NCMEC forwards the report described in clause (i) to—

(I) the requesting foreign law enforcement agency; or

(II) another agency in the same country designated by the Attorney General under paragraph (3) or that has an established relationship with the Federal Bureau of Investigation, U.S. Immigration and Customs Enforcement, or INTERPOL and is involved in the investigation of child sexual exploitation, kidnapping, or enticement crimes.

(B) **Information described.**—The information described in this subparagraph is—

(i) the identity of the foreign law enforcement agency to which the report was forwarded; and

(ii) the date on which the report was forwarded.

(C) **Notification of inability to forward report.**—If a provider notifies NCMEC that the provider is making a report under this section as the result of a request by a foreign law enforcement agency and NCMEC is unable to forward the report as described in subparagraph (A)(ii), NCMEC shall notify the provider that NCMEC was unable to forward the report.

(6) Redesignated (5).

(e) Failure to report.—A provider that knowingly and willfully fails to make a report required under subsection (a)(1) shall be fined—

(1) in the case of an initial knowing and willful failure to make a report, not more than $150,000; and

(2) in the case of any second or subsequent knowing and willful failure to make a report, not more than $300,000.

(f) Protection of privacy.—Nothing in this section shall be construed to require a provider to—

(1) monitor any user, subscriber, or customer of that provider;

(2) monitor the content of any communication of any person described in paragraph (1); or

(3) affirmatively search, screen, or scan for facts or circumstances described in sections (a) and (b).

(g) Conditions of disclosure information contained within report.—

(1) In general.—Except as provided in paragraph (2), a law enforcement agency that receives a report under subsection (c) shall not disclose any information contained in that report.

(2) Permitted disclosures by law enforcement.—

(A) In general.—A law enforcement agency may disclose information in a report received under subsection (c)—

(i) to an attorney for the government for use in the performance of the official duties of that attorney;

(ii) to such officers and employees of that law enforcement agency, as may be necessary in the performance of their investigative and recordkeeping functions;

(iii) to such other government personnel (including personnel of a State or subdivision of a State) as are determined to be necessary by an attorney for the government to assist the attorney in the performance of the official duties of the attorney in enforcing Federal criminal law;

(iv) if the report discloses a violation of State criminal law, to an appropriate official of a State or subdivision of a State for the purpose of enforcing such State law;

(v) to a defendant in a criminal case or the attorney for that defendant, subject to the terms and limitations under section 3509(m) or a similar State law, to the extent the information relates to a criminal charge pending against that defendant;

(vi) subject to subparagraph (B), to a provider if necessary to facilitate response to legal process issued in connection to a criminal investigation, prosecution, or post-conviction remedy relating to that report; and

(vii)   as ordered by a court upon a showing of good cause and pursuant to any protective orders or other conditions that the court may impose.

(B) Limitation.—Nothing   in   subparagraph   (A)(vi) authorizes a law enforcement agency to provide visual depictions of apparent child pornography to a provider.

(3) Permitted disclosures by NCMEC.—NCMEC may disclose by mail, electronic transmission, or other reasonable means, information received in a report under subsection (a) only to—

(A) any Federal law enforcement agency designated by the Attorney General under subsection (d)(2) or that is involved in the investigation of child sexual exploitation, kidnapping, or enticement crimes;

(B) any State, local, or tribal law enforcement agency involved in the investigation of child sexual exploitation, kidnapping, or enticement crimes;

(C) any foreign law enforcement agency designated by the Attorney General under subsection (d)(3) or that has an established relationship with the Federal Bureau of Investigation, Immigration and Customs Enforcement, or INTERPOL, and is involved in the investigation of child sexual exploitation, kidnapping, or enticement crimes;

(D) a provider as described in section 2258C; and

(E) respond to legal process, as necessary.

(4) Permitted disclosure by a provider.—A provider that submits a report under subsection (a)(1) may disclose by mail, electronic transmission, or other reasonable means, information, including visual depictions contained in the report, in a manner consistent with permitted disclosures under paragraphs (3) through (8) of section 2702(b) only to a law enforcement agency described in subparagraph (A), (B), or (C) of paragraph (3), to NCMEC, or as necessary to respond to legal process.

(h) Preservation.—

(1) In general.—For the purposes of this section, a completed submission by a provider of a report to the CyberTipline under subsection (a)(1) shall be treated as a request to preserve the contents provided in the report for 90 days after the submission to the CyberTipline.

(2) Preservation of commingled content.—Pursuant to paragraph (1), a provider shall preserve any visual depictions, data, or other digital files that are reasonably accessible and may provide context or additional information about the reported material or person.

(3) Protection of preserved materials.—A provider preserving materials under this section shall maintain the materials in a secure location and take appropriate steps to limit access by agents or employees of the service to the materials to that access necessary to comply with the requirements of this subsection.

(4) Authorities and duties not affected.—Nothing in this section shall be construed as replacing, amending, or otherwise interfering with the authorities and duties under section 2703.

(5) Redesignated (4).

18 U.S.C. § 2261A. STALKING

Whoever—

(1) travels in interstate or foreign commerce or is present within the special maritime and territorial jurisdiction of the United States, or enters or leaves Indian country, with the intent to kill, injure, harass, intimidate, or place under surveillance with intent to kill, injure, harass, or intimidate another person, and in the course of, or as a result of, such travel or presence engages in conduct that—

(A) places that person in reasonable fear of the death of, or serious bodily injury to—

(i) that person;

(ii) an immediate family member (as defined in section 115) of that person;

(iii) a spouse or intimate partner of that person;

(iv) the pet, service animal, emotional support animal, or horse of that person; or

(B) causes, attempts to cause, or would be reasonably expected to cause substantial emotional distress to a person described in clause (i), (ii), or (iii) of subparagraph (A); or

(2) with the intent to kill, injure, harass, intimidate, or place under surveillance with intent to kill, injure, harass, or intimidate another person, uses the mail, any interactive computer service or electronic communication service or electronic communication system of interstate commerce, or any other facility of interstate or foreign commerce to engage in a course of conduct that—

> **(A)** places that person in reasonable fear of the death of or serious bodily injury to a person, a pet, a service animal, an emotional support animal, or a horse described in clause (i), (ii), (iii), or (iv) of paragraph (1)(A); or

> **(B)** causes, attempts to cause, or would be reasonably expected to cause substantial emotional distress to a person described in clause (i), (ii), or (iii) of paragraph (1)(A),

shall be punished as provided in section 2261(b) or section 2261B, as the case may be.

18 U.S.C. § 2314. TRANSPORTATION OF STOLEN GOODS, SECURITIES, MONEYS, FRAUDULENT STATE TAX STAMPS, OR ARTICLES USED IN COUNTERFEITING

Whoever transports, transmits, or transfers in interstate or foreign commerce any goods, wares, merchandise, securities or money, of the value of $5,000 or more, knowing the same to have been stolen, converted or taken by fraud; or

Whoever, having devised or intending to devise any scheme or artifice to defraud, or for obtaining money or property by means of false or fraudulent pretenses, representations, or promises, transports or causes to be transported, or induces any person or persons to travel in, or to be transported in interstate or foreign commerce in the execution or concealment of a scheme or artifice to defraud that person or those persons of money or property having a value of $5,000 or more; or

Whoever, with unlawful or fraudulent intent, transports in interstate or foreign commerce any falsely made, forged, altered, or counterfeited securities or tax stamps, knowing the same to have been falsely made, forged, altered, or counterfeited; or

Whoever, with unlawful or fraudulent intent, transports in interstate or foreign commerce any traveler's check bearing a forged countersignature; or

Whoever, with unlawful or fraudulent intent, transports in interstate or foreign commerce, any tool, implement, or thing used or fitted to be used in falsely making, forging, altering, or counterfeiting any security or tax stamps, or any part thereof—

Shall be fined under this title or imprisoned not more than ten years, or both.

This section shall not apply to any falsely made, forged, altered, counterfeited or spurious representation of an obligation or other security of the United States, or of an obligation, bond, certificate, security, treasury note, bill, promise to pay or bank note issued by any foreign government. This section also shall not apply to any falsely made, forged, altered, counterfeited, or spurious representation of any bank note or bill issued by a bank or corporation of any foreign country which is intended by the laws or usage of such country to circulate as money.

18 U.S.C. § 2319. CRIMINAL INFRINGEMENT OF A COPYRIGHT

(a) Any person who violates section 506(a) (relating to criminal offenses) of title 17 shall be punished as provided in subsections (b), (c), and (d) and such penalties shall be in addition to any other provisions of title 17 or any other law.

(b) Any person who commits an offense under section 506(a)(1)(A) of title 17—

(1) shall be imprisoned not more than 5 years, or fined in the amount set forth in this title, or both, if the offense consists of the reproduction or distribution, including by electronic means, during any 180-day period, of at least 10 copies or phonorecords, of 1 or more copyrighted works, which have a total retail value of more than $2,500;

(2) shall be imprisoned not more than 10 years, or fined in the amount set forth in this title, or both, if the offense is a felony and is a second or subsequent offense under subsection (a); and

(3) shall be imprisoned not more than 1 year, or fined in the amount set forth in this title, or both, in any other case.

(c) Any person who commits an offense under section 506(a)(1)(B) of title 17—

(1) shall be imprisoned not more than 3 years, or fined in the amount set forth in this title, or both, if the offense consists of the reproduction or distribution of 10 or more copies or phonorecords of 1 or more copyrighted works, which have a total retail value of $2,500 or more;

(2) shall be imprisoned not more than 6 years, or fined in the amount set forth in this title, or both, if the offense is a felony and is a second or subsequent offense under subsection (a); and

(3) shall be imprisoned not more than 1 year, or fined in the amount set forth in this title, or both, if the offense consists of the reproduction or distribution of 1 or more copies or phonorecords of 1 or more copyrighted works, which have a total retail value of more than $1,000.

(d) Any person who commits an offense under section 506(a)(1)(C) of title 17—

(1) shall be imprisoned not more than 3 years, fined under this title, or both;

(2) shall be imprisoned not more than 5 years, fined under this title, or both, if the offense was committed for purposes of commercial advantage or private financial gain;

(3) shall be imprisoned not more than 6 years, fined under this title, or both, if the offense is a felony and is a second or subsequent offense under subsection (a); and

(4) shall be imprisoned not more than 10 years, fined under this title, or both, if the offense is a felony and is a second or subsequent offense under paragraph (2).

(e)(1) During preparation of the presentence report pursuant to Rule 32(c) of the Federal Rules of Criminal Procedure, victims of the offense shall be permitted to submit, and the probation officer shall receive, a victim impact statement that identifies the victim of the offense and the extent and scope of the injury and loss suffered by the victim, including the estimated economic impact of the offense on that victim.

(2) Persons permitted to submit victim impact statements shall include—

(A) producers and sellers of legitimate works affected by conduct involved in the offense;

(B) holders of intellectual property rights in such works; and

(C) the legal representatives of such producers, sellers, and holders.

(f) As used in this section—

(1) the terms "phonorecord" and "copies" have, respectively, the meanings set forth in section 101 (relating to definitions) of title 17;

(2) the terms "reproduction" and "distribution" refer to the exclusive rights of a copyright owner under clauses (1) and (3) respectively of section 106 (relating to exclusive rights in copyrighted works), as limited by sections 107 through 122, of title 17;

(3) the term "financial gain" has the meaning given the term in section 101 of title 17; and

(4) the term "work being prepared for commercial distribution" has the meaning given the term in section 506(a) of title 17.

18 U.S.C. § 2319C. ILLICIT DIGITAL TRANSMISSION SERVICES

(a) **Definitions.** In this section—

(1) the terms "audiovisual work", "computer program", "copies", "copyright owner", "digital transmission", "financial gain", "motion picture", "motion picture exhibition facility", "perform", "phonorecords", "publicly" (with respect to performing a work), "sound recording", and "transmit" have the meanings given those terms in section 101 of title 17;

(2) the term "digital transmission service" means a service that has the primary purpose of publicly performing works by digital transmission;

(3) the terms "publicly perform" and "public performance" refer to the exclusive rights of a copyright owner under paragraphs (4) and (6) of section 106 (relating to exclusive rights in copyrighted works) of title 17, as limited by sections 107 through 122 of title 17; and

(4) the term "work being prepared for commercial public performance" means—

(A) a computer program, a musical work, a motion picture or other audiovisual work, or a sound recording, if, at the time of unauthorized public performance—

(i) the copyright owner has a reasonable expectation of commercial public performance; and

(ii) the copies or phonorecords of the work have not been commercially publicly performed in the United States by or with the authorization of the copyright owner; or

(B) a motion picture, if, at the time of unauthorized public performance, the motion picture—

(i)(I) has been made available for viewing in a motion picture exhibition facility; and

(II) has not been made available in copies for sale to the general public in the United States by or with the authorization of the copyright owner in a format intended to permit viewing outside a motion picture exhibition facility; or

(ii) had not been commercially publicly performed in the United States by or with the authorization of the copyright owner more than 24 hours before the unauthorized public performance.

(b) Prohibited Act. It shall be unlawful for a person to willfully, and for purposes of commercial advantage or private financial gain, offer or provide to the public a digital transmission service that—

(1) is primarily designed or provided for the purpose of publicly performing works protected under title 17 by means of a digital transmission without the authority of the copyright owner or the law;

(2) has no commercially significant purpose or use other than to publicly perform works protected under title 17 by means of a digital transmission without the authority of the copyright owner or the law; or

(3) is intentionally marketed by or at the direction of that person to promote its use in publicly performing works protected under title 17 by means of a digital transmission without the authority of the copyright owner or the law.

(c) Penalties. Any person who violates subsection (b) shall be, in addition to any penalties provided for under title 17 or any other law—

(1) fined under this title, imprisoned not more than 3 years, or both;

(2) fined under this title, imprisoned not more than 5 years, or both, if—

(A) the offense was committed in connection with 1 or more works being prepared for commercial public performance; and

(B) the person knew or should have known that the work was being prepared for commercial public performance; and

(3) fined under this title, imprisoned not more than 10 years, or both, if the offense is a second or subsequent offense under this section or section 2319(a).

(d) Rule of Construction. Nothing in this section shall be construed to—

(1) affect the interpretation of any other provision of civil copyright law, including the limitations of liability set forth in section 512 of title 17, or principles of secondary liability; or

(2) prevent any Federal or State authority from enforcing cable theft or theft of service laws that are not subject to preemption under section 301 of title 17.

17 U.S.C. § 506. CRIMINAL OFFENSES

(a) Criminal infringement.

(1) In general. Any person who willfully infringes a copyright shall be punished as provided under section 2319 of title 18, if the infringement was committed—

(A) for purposes of commercial advantage or private financial gain;

(B) by the reproduction or distribution, including by electronic means, during any 180-day period, of 1 or more copies or phonorecords of 1 or more copyrighted works, which have a total retail value of more than $1,000; or

(C) by the distribution of a work being prepared for commercial distribution, by making it available on a computer network accessible to members of the public, if such person knew or should have known that the work was intended for commercial distribution.

(2) Evidence. For purposes of this subsection, evidence of reproduction or distribution of a copyrighted work, by itself, shall not be sufficient to establish willful infringement of a copyright.

(3) Definition. In this subsection, the term "work being prepared for commercial distribution" means—

(A) a computer program, a musical work, a motion picture or other audiovisual work, or a sound recording, if, at the time of unauthorized distribution—

(i) the copyright owner has a reasonable expectation of commercial distribution; and

(ii) the copies or phonorecords of the work have not been commercially distributed; or

(B) a motion picture, if, at the time of unauthorized distribution, the motion picture—

(i) has been made available for viewing in a motion picture exhibition facility; and

(ii) has not been made available in copies for sale to the general public in the United States in a format intended to permit viewing outside a motion picture exhibition facility.

(b) Forfeiture, destruction, and restitution. Forfeiture, destruction, and restitution relating to this section shall be subject to section 2323 of title 18, to the extent provided in that section, in addition to any other similar remedies provided by law.

(c) Fraudulent Copyright Notice. Any person who, with fraudulent intent, places on any article a notice of copyright or words of the same purport that such person knows to be false, or who, with fraudulent intent, publicly distributes or imports for public distribution any article bearing such notice or words that such person knows to be false, shall be fined not more than $2,500.

(d) Fraudulent Removal of Copyright Notice. Any person who, with fraudulent intent, removes or alters any notice of copyright appearing on a copy of a copyrighted work shall be fined not more than $2,500.

(e) False Representation. Any person who knowingly makes a false representation of a material fact in the application for copyright registration provided for by section 409, or in any written statement filed in connection with the application, shall be fined not more than $2,500.

(f) Rights of Attribution and Integrity. Nothing in this section applies to infringement of the rights conferred by section 106A(a).

18 U.S.C. § 2422. COERCION AND ENTICEMENT

(a) Whoever knowingly persuades, induces, entices, or coerces any individual to travel in interstate or foreign commerce, or in any Territory or Possession of the United States, to engage in prostitution, or in any sexual activity for which any person can be charged with a criminal offense, or attempts to do so, shall be fined under this title or imprisoned not more than 20 years, or both.

(b) Whoever, using the mail or any facility or means of interstate or foreign commerce, or within the special maritime and territorial jurisdiction of the United States knowingly persuades, induces, entices, or coerces any individual who has not attained the age of 18 years, to engage in prostitution or any sexual activity for which any person can be charged with a criminal offense, or attempts to do so, shall be fined under this title and imprisoned not less than 10 years or for life.

18 U.S.C. § 2423. TRANSPORTATION OF MINORS

(a) Transportation with intent to engage in criminal sexual activity. A person who knowingly transports an individual who has not attained the age of 18 years in interstate or foreign commerce, or in any commonwealth, territory or possession of the United States, with intent that the individual engage in prostitution, or in any sexual activity for which any person can be charged with a criminal offense, shall be fined under this title and imprisoned not less than 10 years or for life.

(b) Travel with intent to engage in illicit sexual conduct. A person who travels in interstate commerce or travels into the United States, or a United States citizen or an alien admitted for permanent residence in the United States who travels in foreign commerce, with a motivating purpose of engaging in any illicit sexual conduct with another person shall be fined under this title or imprisoned not more than 30 years, or both.

(c) Engaging in illicit sexual conduct in foreign places. Any United States citizen or alien admitted for permanent residence who travels in foreign commerce, and engages in any illicit sexual conduct with another person shall be fined under this title or imprisoned not more than 30 years, or both.

(d) Ancillary offenses. Whoever, for the purpose of commercial advantage or private financial gain, arranges, induces, procures, or facilitates the travel of a person knowing that such a person is traveling in interstate commerce or foreign commerce with a motivating purpose of engaging in illicit sexual conduct shall be fined under this title, imprisoned not more than 30 years, or both.

(e) Attempt and conspiracy. Whoever attempts or conspires to violate subsection (a), (b), (c), or (d) shall be punishable in the same manner as a completed violation of that subsection.

(f) Definition. As used in this section, the term "illicit sexual conduct" means (1) a sexual act (as defined in section 2246) with a person under 18 years of age that would be in violation of chapter 109A if the sexual act occurred in the special maritime and territorial jurisdiction of the United States; or (2) any commercial sex act (as defined in section 1591) with a person under 18 years of age.

(g) Defense. In a prosecution under this section based on illicit sexual conduct as defined in subsection (f)(2), it is a defense, which the defendant must establish by a preponderance of the evidence, that the defendant reasonably believed that the person with whom the defendant engaged in the commercial sex act had attained the age of 18 years.

18 U.S.C. § 2510. DEFINITIONS

As used in this chapter—

(1) "wire communication" means any aural transfer made in whole or in part through the use of facilities for the transmission of communications by the aid of wire, cable, or other like connection between the point of origin and the point of reception (including the use of such connection in a switching station) furnished or operated by any person engaged in providing or operating such facilities for the transmission of interstate or foreign communications or communications affecting interstate or foreign commerce;

(2) "oral communication" means any oral communication uttered by a person exhibiting an expectation that such communication is not subject to interception under circumstances justifying such expectation, but such term does not include any electronic communication;

(3) "State" means any State of the United States, the District of Columbia, the Commonwealth of Puerto Rico, and any territory or possession of the United States;

(4) "intercept" means the aural or other acquisition of the contents of any wire, electronic, or oral communication through the use of any electronic, mechanical, or other device.

(5) "electronic, mechanical, or other device" means any device or apparatus which can be used to intercept a wire, oral, or electronic communication other than—

   (A) any telephone or telegraph instrument, equipment or facility, or any component thereof, (i) furnished to the subscriber or user by a provider of wire or electronic communication service in the ordinary course of its business and being used by the subscriber or user in the ordinary course of its business or furnished by such subscriber or user for connection to the facilities of such service and used in the ordinary course of its business; or (ii) being used by a provider of wire or electronic communication service in the ordinary course of its business, or by an investigative or law enforcement officer in the ordinary course of his duties;

   (B) a hearing aid or similar device being used to correct subnormal hearing to not better than normal;

(6) "person" means any employee, or agent of the United States or any State or political subdivision thereof, and any individual, partnership, association, joint stock company, trust, or corporation;

(7) "Investigative or law enforcement officer" means any officer of the United States or of a State or political subdivision thereof, who is empowered by law to conduct investigations of or to make arrests for offenses enumerated in this chapter, and any attorney authorized by law to prosecute or participate in the prosecution of such offenses;

(8) "contents", when used with respect to any wire, oral, or electronic communication, includes any information concerning the substance, purport, or meaning of that communication;

(9) "Judge of competent jurisdiction" means—

   (A) a judge of a United States district court or a United States court of appeals; and

   (B) a judge of any court of general criminal jurisdiction of a State who is authorized by a statute of that State to enter orders authorizing interceptions of wire, oral, or electronic communications;

(10) "communication common carrier" has the meaning given that term in section 3 of the Communications Act of 1934;

(11) "aggrieved person" means a person who was a party to any intercepted wire, oral, or electronic communication or a person against whom the interception was directed;

(12) "electronic communication" means any transfer of signs, signals, writing, images, sounds, data, or intelligence of any nature transmitted in whole or in part by a wire, radio, electromagnetic, photoelectronic or photooptical system that affects interstate or foreign commerce, but does not include—

    (A) any wire or oral communication;

    (B) any communication made through a tone-only paging device;

    (C) any communication from a tracking device (as defined in section 3117 of this title); or

    (D) electronic funds transfer information stored by a financial institution in a communications system used for the electronic storage and transfer of funds;

(13) "user" means any person or entity who—

    (A) uses an electronic communication service; and

    (B) is duly authorized by the provider of such service to engage in such use;

(14) "electronic communications system" means any wire, radio, electromagnetic, photooptical or photoelectronic facilities for the transmission of wire or electronic communications, and any computer facilities or related electronic equipment for the electronic storage of such communications;

(15) "electronic communication service" means any service which provides to users thereof the ability to send or receive wire or electronic communications;

(16) "readily accessible to the general public" means, with respect to a radio communication, that such communication is not—

    (A) scrambled or encrypted;

    (B) transmitted using modulation techniques whose essential parameters have been withheld from the public with the intention of preserving the privacy of such communication;

(C) carried on a subcarrier or other signal subsidiary to a radio transmission;

(D) transmitted over a communication system provided by a common carrier, unless the communication is a tone only paging system communication; or

(E) transmitted on frequencies allocated under part 25, subpart D, E, or F of part 74, or part 94 of the Rules of the Federal Communications Commission, unless, in the case of a communication transmitted on a frequency allocated under part 74 that is not exclusively allocated to broadcast auxiliary services, the communication is a two-way voice communication by radio;

(17) "electronic storage" means—

(A) any temporary, intermediate storage of a wire or electronic communication incidental to the electronic transmission thereof; and

(B) any storage of such communication by an electronic communication service for purposes of backup protection of such communication;

(18) "aural transfer" means a transfer containing the human voice at any point between and including the point of origin and the point of reception;

(19) "foreign intelligence information", for purposes of section 2517(6) of this title, means—

(A) information, whether or not concerning a United States person, that relates to the ability of the United States to protect against—

(i) actual or potential attack or other grave hostile acts of a foreign power or an agent of a foreign power;

(ii) sabotage or international terrorism by a foreign power or an agent of a foreign power; or

(iii) clandestine intelligence activities by an intelligence service or network of a foreign power or by an agent of a foreign power; or

(B) information, whether or not concerning a United States person, with respect to a foreign power or foreign territory that relates to—

(i) the national defense or the security of the United States; or

(ii) the conduct of the foreign affairs of the United States;

(20) "protected computer" has the meaning set forth in section 1030; and

(21) "computer trespasser"—

(A) means a person who accesses a protected computer without authorization and thus has no reasonable expectation of privacy in any communication transmitted to, through, or from the protected computer; and

(B) does not include a person known by the owner or operator of the protected computer to have an existing contractual relationship with the owner or operator of the protected computer for access to all or part of the protected computer.

18 U.S.C. § 2511. INTERCEPTION AND DISCLOSURE OF WIRE, ORAL, OR ELECTRONIC COMMUNICATIONS PROHIBITED

(1) Except as otherwise specifically provided in this chapter any person who—

(a) intentionally intercepts, endeavors to intercept, or procures any other person to intercept or endeavor to intercept, any wire, oral, or electronic communication;

(b) intentionally uses, endeavors to use, or procures any other person to use or endeavor to use any electronic, mechanical, or other device to intercept any oral communication when—

(i) such device is affixed to, or otherwise transmits a signal through, a wire, cable, or other like connection used in wire communication; or

(ii) such device transmits communications by radio, or interferes with the transmission of such communication; or

(iii) such person knows, or has reason to know, that such device or any component thereof has been sent through the mail or transported in interstate or foreign commerce; or

(iv) such use or endeavor to use (A) takes place on the premises of any business or other commercial establishment the operations of which affect interstate or foreign commerce; or (B) obtains or is for the purpose of obtaining information relating to the operations of any business or other commercial establishment the operations of which affect interstate or foreign commerce; or

(v) such person acts in the District of Columbia, the Commonwealth of Puerto Rico, or any territory or possession of the United States;

(c) intentionally discloses, or endeavors to disclose, to any other person the contents of any wire, oral, or electronic communication, knowing or having reason to know that the information was obtained through the interception of a wire, oral, or electronic communication in violation of this subsection;

(d) intentionally uses, or endeavors to use, the contents of any wire, oral, or electronic communication, knowing or having reason to know that the information was obtained through the interception of a wire, oral, or electronic communication in violation of this subsection; or

(e)(i) intentionally discloses, or endeavors to disclose, to any other person the contents of any wire, oral, or electronic communication, intercepted by means authorized by sections 2511(2)(a)(ii), 2511(2)(b)–(c), 2511(2)(e), 2516, and 2518 of this chapter, (ii) knowing or having reason to know that the information was obtained through the interception of such a communication in connection with a criminal investigation, (iii) having obtained or received the information in connection with a criminal investigation, and (iv) with intent to improperly obstruct, impede, or interfere with a duly authorized criminal investigation,

shall be punished as provided in subsection (4) or shall be subject to suit as provided in subsection (5).

(2)(a)(i) It shall not be unlawful under this chapter for an operator of a switchboard, or an officer, employee, or agent of a provider of wire or electronic communication service, whose facilities are used in the transmission of a wire or electronic communication, to intercept, disclose, or use that communication in the normal course of his employment while engaged in any activity which is a necessary incident to the rendition of his service or to the protection of the rights or property of the provider of that service, except that a provider of wire communication service to the public shall not utilize service observing or random monitoring except for mechanical or service quality control checks.

(ii) Notwithstanding any other law, providers of wire or electronic communication service, their officers, employees, and agents, landlords, custodians, or other persons, are authorized to provide information, facilities, or technical assistance to persons authorized by law to intercept wire, oral, or electronic communications or to conduct electronic surveillance, as defined in section 101 of the Foreign Intelligence Surveillance Act of 1978, if such provider, its officers, employees, or agents, landlord, custodian, or other specified person, has been provided with—

(A) a court order directing such assistance or a court order pursuant to section 704 of the Foreign Intelligence Surveillance Act of 1978 signed by the authorizing judge, or

(B) a certification in writing by a person specified in section 2518(7) of this title or the Attorney General of the United States that no warrant or court order is required by law, that all statutory requirements have been met, and that the specified assistance is required,

setting forth period of time during which the provision of the information, facilities, or technical assistance is authorized and specifying the information, facilities, or technical assistance required. No provider of wire or electronic communication service, officer, employee, or agent thereof, or landlord, custodian, or other specified person shall disclose the existence of any interception or surveillance or the device used to accomplish the interception or surveillance with respect to which the person has been furnished a court order or certification under this chapter, except as may otherwise be required by legal process and then only after prior notification to the Attorney General or to the principal prosecuting attorney of a State or any political subdivision of a State, as may be appropriate. Any such disclosure, shall render such person liable for the civil damages provided for in section 2520. No cause of action shall lie in any court against any provider of wire or electronic communication service, its officers, employees, or agents, landlord, custodian, or other specified person for providing information, facilities, or assistance in accordance with the terms of a court order, statutory authorization, or certification under this chapter.

(iii) If a certification under subparagraph (ii)(B) for assistance to obtain foreign intelligence information is based on statutory authority, the certification shall identify the specific statutory provision and shall certify that the statutory requirements have been met.

(b) It shall not be unlawful under this chapter for an officer, employee, or agent of the Federal Communications Commission, in the normal course of his employment and in discharge of the monitoring responsibilities exercised by the Commission in the enforcement of chapter 5 of title 47 of the United States Code, to intercept a wire or electronic communication, or oral communication transmitted by radio, or to disclose or use the information thereby obtained.

(c) It shall not be unlawful under this chapter for a person acting under color of law to intercept a wire, oral, or electronic communication, where such person is a party to the communication or one of the parties to the communication has given prior consent to such interception.

(d) It shall not be unlawful under this chapter for a person not acting under color of law to intercept a wire, oral, or electronic communication where such person is a party to the communication or where one of the parties to the communication has given prior consent to such interception unless such communication is intercepted for the purpose of committing any criminal or tortious act in violation of the Constitution or laws of the United States or of any State.

(e) Notwithstanding any other provision of this title or section 705 or 706 of the Communications Act of 1934, it shall not be unlawful for an officer, employee, or agent of the United States in the normal course of his official duty to conduct electronic surveillance, as defined in section 101 of the Foreign Intelligence Surveillance Act of 1978, as authorized by that Act.

(f) Nothing contained in this chapter or chapter 121 or 206 of this title, or section 705 of the Communications Act of 1934, shall be deemed to affect the acquisition by the United States Government of foreign intelligence information from international or foreign communications, or foreign intelligence activities conducted in accordance with otherwise applicable Federal law involving a foreign electronic communications system, utilizing a means other than electronic surveillance as defined in section 101 of the Foreign Intelligence Surveillance Act of 1978, and procedures in this chapter or chapter 121 and the Foreign Intelligence Surveillance Act of 1978 shall be the exclusive means by which electronic surveillance, as defined in section 101 of such Act, and the interception of domestic wire, oral, and electronic communications may be conducted.

(g) It shall not be unlawful under this chapter or chapter 121 of this title for any person—

(i) to intercept or access an electronic communication made through an electronic communication system that is configured so that such electronic communication is readily accessible to the general public;

(ii) to intercept any radio communication which is transmitted—

(I) by any station for the use of the general public, or that relates to ships, aircraft, vehicles, or persons in distress;

(II) by any governmental, law enforcement, civil defense, private land mobile, or public safety communications system, including police and fire, readily accessible to the general public;

(III) by a station operating on an authorized frequency within the bands allocated to the amateur, citizens band, or general mobile radio services; or

(IV) by any marine or aeronautical communications system;

(iii) to engage in any conduct which—

(I)   is prohibited by section 633 of the Communications Act of 1934; or

(II)   is excepted from the application of section 705(a) of the Communications Act of 1934 by section 705(b) of that Act;

(iv) to intercept any wire or electronic communication the transmission of which is causing harmful interference to any lawfully operating station or consumer electronic equipment, to the extent necessary to identify the source of such interference; or

(v) for other users of the same frequency to intercept any radio communication made through a system that utilizes frequencies monitored by individuals engaged in the provision or the use of such system, if such communication is not scrambled or encrypted.

(h)   It shall not be unlawful under this chapter—

(i)   to use a pen register or a trap and trace device (as those terms are defined for the purposes of chapter 206 (relating to pen registers and trap and trace devices) of this title); or

(ii) for a provider of electronic communication service to record the fact that a wire or electronic communication was initiated or completed in order to protect such provider, another provider furnishing service toward the completion of the wire or electronic communication, or a user of that service, from fraudulent, unlawful or abusive use of such service.

(i)   It shall not be unlawful under this chapter for a person acting under color of law to intercept the wire or electronic communications of a computer trespasser transmitted to, through, or from the protected computer, if—

(I)   the owner or operator of the protected computer authorizes the interception of the computer trespasser's communications on the protected computer;

(II)   the person acting under color of law is lawfully engaged in an investigation;

(III) the person acting under color of law has reasonable grounds to believe that the contents of the computer trespasser's communications will be relevant to the investigation; and

(IV) such interception does not acquire communications other than those transmitted to or from the computer trespasser.

(j) It shall not be unlawful under this chapter for a provider of electronic communication service to the public or remote computing service to intercept or disclose the contents of a wire or electronic communication in response to an order from a foreign government that is subject to an executive agreement that the Attorney General has determined and certified to Congress satisfies section 2523.

(3)(a) Except as provided in paragraph (b) of this subsection, a person or entity providing an electronic communication service to the public shall not intentionally divulge the contents of any communication (other than one to such person or entity, or an agent thereof) while in transmission on that service to any person or entity other than an addressee or intended recipient of such communication or an agent of such addressee or intended recipient.

(b) A person or entity providing electronic communication service to the public may divulge the contents of any such communication—

(i) as otherwise authorized in section 2511(2)(a) or 2517 of this title;

(ii) with the lawful consent of the originator or any addressee or intended recipient of such communication;

(iii) to a person employed or authorized, or whose facilities are used, to forward such communication to its destination; or

(iv) which were inadvertently obtained by the service provider and which appear to pertain to the commission of a crime, if such divulgence is made to a law enforcement agency.

(4)(a) Except as provided in paragraph (b) of this subsection or in subsection (5), whoever violates subsection (1) of this section shall be fined under this title or imprisoned not more than five years, or both.

(b) Conduct otherwise an offense under this subsection that consists of or relates to the interception of a satellite transmission that is not encrypted or scrambled and that is transmitted—

(i) to a broadcasting station for purposes of retransmission to the general public; or

(ii) as an audio subcarrier intended for redistribution to facilities open to the public, but not including data transmissions or telephone calls, is not an offense under this subsection unless the conduct is for the purposes of direct or indirect commercial advantage or private financial gain.

(5)(a)(i) If the communication is—

(A) a private satellite video communication that is not scrambled or encrypted and the conduct in violation of this chapter is the private viewing of that communication and is not for a tortious or illegal purpose or for purposes of direct or indirect commercial advantage or private commercial gain; or

(B) a radio communication that is transmitted on frequencies allocated under subpart D of part 74 of the rules of the Federal Communications Commission that is not scrambled or encrypted and the conduct in violation of this chapter is not for a tortious or illegal purpose or for purposes of direct or indirect commercial advantage or private commercial gain,

then the person who engages in such conduct shall be subject to suit by the Federal Government in a court of competent jurisdiction.

(ii) In an action under this subsection—

(A) if the violation of this chapter is a first offense for the person under paragraph (a) of subsection (4) and such person has not been found liable in a civil action under section 2520 of this title, the Federal Government shall be entitled to appropriate injunctive relief; and

(B) if the violation of this chapter is a second or subsequent offense under paragraph (a) of subsection (4) or such person has been found liable in any prior civil action under section 2520, the person shall be subject to a mandatory $500 civil fine.

(b) The court may use any means within its authority to enforce an injunction issued under paragraph (ii)(A), and shall impose a civil fine of not less than $500 for each violation of such an injunction.

18 U.S.C. § 2512. MANUFACTURE, DISTRIBUTION, POSSESSION, AND ADVERTISING OF WIRE, ORAL, OR ELECTRONIC COMMUNICATION INTERCEPTING DEVICES PROHIBITED

(1) Except as otherwise specifically provided in this chapter, any person who intentionally—

(a) sends through the mail, or sends or carries in interstate or foreign commerce, any electronic, mechanical, or other device, knowing or having reason to know that the design of such device renders it primarily useful for the purpose of the surreptitious interception of wire, oral, or electronic communications;

(b) manufactures, assembles, possesses, or sells any electronic, mechanical, or other device, knowing or having reason to know that the design of such device renders it primarily useful for the purpose of the surreptitious interception of wire, oral, or electronic communications, and that such device or any component thereof has been or will be sent through the mail or transported in interstate or foreign commerce; or

(c) places in any newspaper, magazine, handbill, or other publication or disseminates by electronic means any advertisement of—

    (i) any electronic, mechanical, or other device knowing the content of the advertisement and knowing or having reason to know that the design of such device renders it primarily useful for the purpose of the surreptitious interception of wire, oral, or electronic communications; or

    (ii) any other electronic, mechanical, or other device, where such advertisement promotes the use of such device for the purpose of the surreptitious interception of wire, oral, or electronic communications,

knowing the content of the advertisement and knowing or having reason to know that such advertisement will be sent through the mail or transported in interstate or foreign commerce,

shall be fined under this title or imprisoned not more than five years, or both.

(2) It shall not be unlawful under this section for—

(a) a provider of wire or electronic communication service or an officer, agent, or employee of, or a person under contract with, such a provider, in the normal course of the business of providing that wire or electronic communication service, or

(b) an officer, agent, or employee of, or a person under contract with, the United States, a State, or a political subdivision thereof, in the normal course of the activities of the United States, a State, or a political subdivision thereof,

to send through the mail, send or carry in interstate or foreign commerce, or manufacture, assemble, possess, or sell any electronic, mechanical, or other device knowing or having reason to know that the design of such device renders it primarily useful for the purpose of the surreptitious interception of wire, oral, or electronic communications.

(3) It shall not be unlawful under this section to advertise for sale a device described in subsection (1) of this section if the advertisement is mailed, sent, or carried in interstate or foreign commerce solely to a domestic provider of wire or electronic communication service or to an agency of the United States, a State, or a political subdivision thereof which is duly authorized to use such device.

18 U.S.C. § 2513. CONFISCATION OF WIRE, ORAL, OR ELECTRONIC COMMUNICATION INTERCEPTING DEVICES

Any electronic, mechanical, or other device used, sent, carried, manufactured, assembled, possessed, sold, or advertised in violation of section 2511 or section 2512 of this chapter may be seized and forfeited to the United States. All provisions of law relating to (1) the seizure, summary and judicial forfeiture, and condemnation of vessels, vehicles, merchandise, and baggage for violations of the customs laws contained in title 19 of the United States Code, (2) the disposition of such vessels, vehicles, merchandise, and baggage or the proceeds from the sale thereof, (3) the remission or mitigation of such forfeiture, (4) the compromise of claims, and (5) the award of compensation to informers in respect of such forfeitures, shall apply to seizures and forfeitures incurred, or alleged to have been incurred, under the provisions of this section, insofar as applicable and not inconsistent with the provisions of this section; except that such duties as are imposed upon the collector of customs or any other person with respect to the seizure and forfeiture of vessels, vehicles, merchandise, and baggage under the provisions of the customs laws contained in title 19 of the United States Code shall be performed with respect to seizure and forfeiture of electronic, mechanical, or other intercepting devices under this section by such officers, agents, or other persons as may be authorized or designated for that purpose by the Attorney General.

18 U.S.C. § 2515. PROHIBITION OF USE AS EVIDENCE OF INTERCEPTED WIRE OR ORAL COMMUNICATIONS

Whenever any wire or oral communication has been intercepted, no part of the contents of such communication and no evidence derived therefrom may be received in evidence in any trial, hearing, or other proceeding in or before any court, grand jury, department, officer, agency, regulatory body, legislative committee, or other authority of the United States, a State, or a political subdivision thereof if the disclosure of that information would be in violation of this chapter.

18 U.S.C. § 2516. AUTHORIZATION FOR INTERCEPTION OF WIRE, ORAL, OR ELECTRONIC COMMUNICATIONS

(1) The Attorney General, Deputy Attorney General, Associate Attorney General, or any Assistant Attorney General, any acting Assistant Attorney General, or any Deputy Assistant Attorney General or acting Deputy Assistant Attorney General in the Criminal Division or National

Security Division specially designated by the Attorney General, may authorize an application to a Federal judge of competent jurisdiction for, and such judge may grant in conformity with section 2518 of this chapter an order authorizing or approving the interception of wire or oral communications by the Federal Bureau of Investigation, or a Federal agency having responsibility for the investigation of the offense as to which the application is made, when such interception may provide or has provided evidence of—

(a) any offense punishable by death or by imprisonment for more than one year under sections 2122 and 2274 through 2277 of title 42 of the United States Code (relating to the enforcement of the Atomic Energy Act of 1954), section 2284 of title 42 of the United States Code (relating to sabotage of nuclear facilities or fuel), or under the following chapters of this title: chapter 10 (relating to biological weapons), chapter 37 (relating to espionage), chapter 55 (relating to kidnapping), chapter 90 (relating to protection of trade secrets), chapter 105 (relating to sabotage), chapter 115 (relating to treason), chapter 102 (relating to riots), chapter 65 (relating to malicious mischief), chapter 111 (relating to destruction of vessels), or chapter 81 (relating to piracy);

(b) a violation of section 186 or section 501(c) of title 29, United States Code (dealing with restrictions on payments and loans to labor organizations), or any offense which involves murder, kidnapping, robbery, or extortion, and which is punishable under this title;

(c) any offense which is punishable under the following sections of this title: section 37 (relating to violence at international airports), section 43 (relating to animal enterprise terrorism), section 81 (arson within special maritime and territorial jurisdiction), section 201 (bribery of public officials and witnesses), section 215 (relating to bribery of bank officials), section 224 (bribery in sporting contests), subsection (d), (e), (f), (g), (h), or (i) of section 844 (unlawful use of explosives), section 1032 (relating to concealment of assets), section 1084 (transmission of wagering information), section 751 (relating to escape), section 832 (relating to nuclear and weapons of mass destruction threats), section 842 (relating to explosive materials), section 930 (relating to possession of weapons in Federal facilities), section 1014 (relating to loans and credit applications generally; renewals and discounts), section 1114 (relating to officers and employees of the United States), section 1116 (relating to protection of foreign officials), sections 1503, 1512, and 1513 (influencing or injuring an officer, juror, or witness generally), section 1510 (obstruction of criminal investigations), section 1511 (obstruction of State or local law enforcement), section 1581 (peonage), section 1582 (vessels for slave trade), section 1583 (enticement into slavery), section 1584 (involuntary servitude), section 1585 (seizure, detention, transportation or sale of slaves), section 1586 (service on vessels in slave trade), section 1587 (possession of slaves aboard vessel), section 1588 (transportation of slaves from United States), section 1589 (forced labor), section 1590 (trafficking with respect to peonage, slavery, involuntary servitude, or forced labor), section 1591 (sex trafficking of children by force, fraud, or coercion), section 1592 (unlawful conduct with respect to documents in furtherance of trafficking, peonage, slavery, involuntary servitude, or forced labor), section 1751 (Presidential and Presidential staff assassination, kidnapping, and assault), section 1951 (interference with commerce by threats or violence), section 1952 (interstate and foreign travel or transportation in aid of racketeering enterprises), section 1958 (relating to use of interstate commerce facilities in the commission of murder for hire), section 1959 (relating to violent crimes in aid of racketeering activity), section 1954 (offer, acceptance, or solicitation to influence operations of employee benefit plan), section 1955 (prohibition of business enterprises of gambling), section 1956 (laundering of monetary instruments), section 1957 (relating to engaging in monetary transactions in property derived from specified unlawful activity), section 659 (theft from interstate shipment), section 664 (embezzlement from pension and welfare funds), section 1343 (fraud by wire, radio, or television), section 1344 (relating to bank fraud), section 1992 (relating to terrorist attacks against mass transportation), sections 2251 and 2252 (sexual exploitation of children), section 2251A (selling or buying of children), section 2252A (relating to material constituting or containing child pornography), section 1466A (relating to child obscenity), section 2260 (production of sexually explicit depictions of a minor for importation into the United States), sections 2421, 2422, 2423, and 2425 (relating to transportation for illegal sexual activity and related crimes), sections 2312, 2313, 2314, and 2315 (interstate transportation of stolen property), section 2321 (relating to trafficking in certain motor vehicles or motor vehicle parts), section 2340A (relating to torture), section 1203 (relating to hostage taking), section 1029 (relating to fraud and related activity in connection with access devices), section 3146 (relating to penalty for failure to appear), section 3521(b)(3) (relating to witness relocation and assistance), section 32 (relating to destruction of aircraft or aircraft facilities), section 38 (relating to aircraft parts fraud), section 1963 (violations with respect to racketeer influenced and corrupt organizations), section 115 (relating to threatening or retaliating against a Federal official), section 1341 (relating to mail fraud), a felony violation of section 1030 (relating to computer fraud and abuse), section 351 (violations with respect to congressional, Cabinet, or Supreme Court assassinations, kidnapping, and assault), section 831 (relating to prohibited transactions involving nuclear materials), section 33 (relating to destruction of motor vehicles or motor vehicle facilities), section 175 (relating to biological weapons), section 175c (relating to variola virus), section 956 (conspiracy to harm persons or property overseas), a felony violation of section 1028 (relating to production of false identification documentation), section 1425 (relating to the procurement of citizenship or nationalization unlawfully), section 1426 (relating to the reproduction of naturalization or citizenship papers), section 1427 (relating to the sale of naturalization or citizenship papers), section 1541 (relating to passport issuance without authority), section 1542 (relating to false statements in passport applications), section 1543 (relating to forgery or false use of passports), section 1544 (relating to misuse of passports), section 1546 (relating to fraud and misuse of visas, permits, and other documents), or section 555 (relating to construction or use of international border tunnels);

(d) any offense involving counterfeiting punishable under section 471, 472, or 473 of this title;

(e) any offense involving fraud connected with a case under title 11 or the manufacture, importation, receiving, concealment, buying, selling, or otherwise dealing in narcotic drugs, marihuana, or other dangerous drugs, punishable under any law of the United States;

(f) any offense including extortionate credit transactions under sections 892, 893, or 894 of this title;

(g) a violation of section 5322 of title 31, United States Code (dealing with the reporting of currency transactions), or section 5324 of title 31, United States Code (relating to structuring transactions to evade reporting requirement prohibited);

(h) any felony violation of sections 2511 and 2512 (relating to interception and disclosure of certain communications and to certain intercepting devices) of this title;

(i) any felony violation of chapter 71 (relating to obscenity) of this title;

(j) any violation of section 60123(b) (relating to destruction of a natural gas pipeline), section 46502 (relating to aircraft piracy), the second sentence of section 46504 (relating to assault on a flight crew with dangerous weapon), or section 46505(b)(3) or (c) (relating to explosive or incendiary devices, or endangerment of human life, by means of weapons on aircraft) of title 49;

(k) any criminal violation of section 2778 of title 22 (relating to the Arms Export Control Act);

(*l*) the location of any fugitive from justice from an offense described in this section;

(**m**) a violation of section 274, 277, or 278 of the Immigration and Nationality Act (8 U.S.C. 1324, 1327, or 1328) (relating to the smuggling of aliens);

(**n**) any felony violation of sections 922 and 924 of title 18, United States Code (relating to firearms);

(**o**) any violation of section 5861 of the Internal Revenue Code of 1986 (relating to firearms);

(**p**) a felony violation of section 1028 (relating to production of false identification documents), section 1542 (relating to false statements in passport applications), section 1546 (relating to fraud and misuse of visas, permits, and other documents), section 1028A (relating to aggravated identity theft) of this title or a violation of section 274, 277, or 278 of the Immigration and Nationality Act (relating to the smuggling of aliens); or

(**q**) any criminal violation of section 229 (relating to chemical weapons) or section 2332, 2332a, 2332b, 2332d, 2332f, 2332g, 2332h3 2339, 2339A, 2339B, 2339C, or 2339D of this title (relating to terrorism);

(**r**) any criminal violation of section 1 (relating to illegal restraints of trade or commerce), 2 (relating to illegal monopolizing of trade or commerce), or 3 (relating to illegal restraints of trade or commerce in territories or the District of Columbia) of the Sherman Act (15 U.S.C. 1, 2, 3);

(**s**) any violation of section 670 (relating to theft of medical products);

(**t**) any violation of the Export Control Reform Act of 2018; or

(**u**) any conspiracy to commit any offense described in any subparagraph of this paragraph.

(**2**) The principal prosecuting attorney of any State, or the principal prosecuting attorney of any political subdivision thereof, if such attorney is authorized by a statute of that State to make application to a State court judge of competent jurisdiction for an order authorizing or approving the interception of wire, oral, or electronic communications, may apply to such judge for, and such judge may grant in conformity with section 2518 of this chapter and with the applicable State statute an order authorizing, or approving the interception of wire, oral, or electronic communications by investigative or law enforcement officers having responsibility for the investigation of the offense as to which the application is made, when such interception may provide or has provided evidence of the commission of the offense of murder, kidnapping, human trafficking, child sexual exploitation, child pornography production, prostitution, gambling, robbery, bribery, extortion, or dealing in narcotic drugs, marihuana or other dangerous drugs, or other crime dangerous to life, limb, or property, and punishable by imprisonment for more than one year, designated in any applicable State statute authorizing such interception, or any conspiracy to commit any of the foregoing offenses.

(3) Any attorney for the Government (as such term is defined for the purposes of the Federal Rules of Criminal Procedure) may authorize an application to a Federal judge of competent jurisdiction for, and such judge may grant, in conformity with section 2518 of this title, an order authorizing or approving the interception of electronic communications by an investigative or law enforcement officer having responsibility for the investigation of the offense as to which the application is made, when such interception may provide or has provided evidence of any Federal felony.

18 U.S.C. § 2517. AUTHORIZATION FOR DISCLOSURE AND USE OF INTERCEPTED WIRE, ORAL, OR ELECTRONIC COMMUNICATIONS

(1) Any investigative or law enforcement officer who, by any means authorized by this chapter, has obtained knowledge of the contents of any wire, oral, or electronic communication, or evidence derived therefrom, may disclose such contents to another investigative or law enforcement officer to the extent that such disclosure is appropriate to the proper performance of the official duties of the officer making or receiving the disclosure.

(2) Any investigative or law enforcement officer who, by any means authorized by this chapter, has obtained knowledge of the contents of any wire, oral, or electronic communication or evidence derived therefrom may use such contents to the extent such use is appropriate to the proper performance of his official duties.

(3) Any person who has received, by any means authorized by this chapter, any information concerning a wire, oral, or electronic communication, or evidence derived therefrom intercepted in accordance with the provisions of this chapter may disclose the contents of that communication or such derivative evidence while giving testimony under oath or affirmation in any proceeding held under the authority of the United States or of any State or political subdivision thereof.

(4) No otherwise privileged wire, oral, or electronic communication intercepted in accordance with, or in violation of, the provisions of this chapter shall lose its privileged character.

(5) When an investigative or law enforcement officer, while engaged in intercepting wire, oral, or electronic communications in the manner authorized herein, intercepts wire, oral, or electronic communications relating to offenses other than those specified in the order of authorization or approval, the contents thereof, and evidence derived therefrom, may be disclosed or used as provided in subsections (1) and (2) of this section. Such contents and any evidence derived therefrom may be used under subsection (3) of this section when authorized or approved by a judge of competent jurisdiction where such judge finds on subsequent application that the contents were otherwise intercepted in accordance with the provisions of this chapter. Such application shall be made as soon as practicable.

(6) Any investigative or law enforcement officer, or attorney for the Government, who by any means authorized by this chapter, has obtained knowledge of the contents of any wire, oral, or electronic communication, or evidence derived therefrom, may disclose such contents to any other Federal law enforcement, intelligence, protective, immigration, national defense, or national security official to the extent that such contents include foreign intelligence or counterintelligence (as defined in section 3 of the National Security Act of 1947 (50 U.S.C. 401a)), or foreign intelligence information (as defined in subsection (19) of section 2510 of this title), to assist the official who is to receive that information in the performance of his official duties. Any Federal official who receives information pursuant to this provision may use that information only as necessary in the conduct of that person's official duties subject to any limitations on the unauthorized disclosure of such information.

(7) Any investigative or law enforcement officer, or other Federal official in carrying out official duties as such Federal official, who by any means authorized by this chapter, has obtained knowledge of the contents of any wire, oral, or electronic communication, or evidence derived therefrom, may disclose such contents or derivative evidence to a foreign investigative or law enforcement officer to the extent that such disclosure is appropriate to the proper performance of the official duties of the officer making or receiving the disclosure, and foreign investigative or law enforcement officers may use or disclose such contents or derivative evidence to the extent such use or disclosure is appropriate to the proper performance of their official duties.

(8) Any investigative or law enforcement officer, or other Federal official in carrying out official duties as such Federal official, who by any means authorized by this chapter, has obtained knowledge of the contents of any wire, oral, or electronic communication, or evidence derived therefrom, may disclose such contents or derivative evidence to any appropriate Federal, State, local, or foreign government official to the extent that such contents or derivative evidence reveals a threat of actual or potential attack or other grave hostile acts of a foreign power or an agent of a foreign power, domestic or international sabotage, domestic or international terrorism, or clandestine intelligence gathering activities by an intelligence service or network of a foreign power or by an agent of a foreign power, within the United States or elsewhere, for the purpose of

preventing or responding to such a threat. Any official who receives information pursuant to this provision may use that information only as necessary in the conduct of that person's official duties subject to any limitations on the unauthorized disclosure of such information, and any State, local, or foreign official who receives information pursuant to this provision may use that information only consistent with such guidelines as the Attorney General and Director of Central Intelligence shall jointly issue.

18 U.S.C. § 2518. PROCEDURE FOR INTERCEPTION OF WIRE, ORAL, OR ELECTRONIC COMMUNICATIONS

(1) Each application for an order authorizing or approving the interception of a wire, oral, or electronic communication under this chapter shall be made in writing upon oath or affirmation to a judge of competent jurisdiction and shall state the applicant's authority to make such application. Each application shall include the following information:

(a) the identity of the investigative or law enforcement officer making the application, and the officer authorizing the application;

(b) a full and complete statement of the facts and circumstances relied upon by the applicant, to justify his belief that an order should be issued, including (i) details as to the particular offense that has been, is being, or is about to be committed, (ii) except as provided in subsection (11), a particular description of the nature and location of the facilities from which or the place where the communication is to be intercepted, (iii) a particular description of the type of communications sought to be intercepted, (iv) the identity of the person, if known, committing the offense and whose communications are to be intercepted;

(c) a full and complete statement as to whether or not other investigative procedures have been tried and failed or why they reasonably appear to be unlikely to succeed if tried or to be too dangerous;

(d) a statement of the period of time for which the interception is required to be maintained. If the nature of the investigation is such that the authorization for interception should not automatically terminate when the described type of communication has been first obtained, a particular description of facts establishing probable cause to believe that additional communications of the same type will occur thereafter;

(e) a full and complete statement of the facts concerning all previous applications known to the individual authorizing and making the application, made to any judge for authorization to intercept, or for approval of interceptions of, wire, oral, or electronic communications involving any of the same persons, facilities or places specified in the application, and the action taken by the judge on each such application; and

(f) where the application is for the extension of an order, a statement setting forth the results thus far obtained from the interception, or a reasonable explanation of the failure to obtain such results.

(2) The judge may require the applicant to furnish additional testimony or documentary evidence in support of the application.

(3) Upon such application the judge may enter an ex parte order, as requested or as modified, authorizing or approving interception of wire, oral, or electronic communications within the territorial jurisdiction of the court in which the judge is sitting (and outside that jurisdiction but within the United States in the case of a mobile interception device authorized by a Federal court within such jurisdiction), if the judge determines on the basis of the facts submitted by the applicant that—

(a) there is probable cause for belief that an individual is committing, has committed, or is about to commit a particular offense enumerated in section 2516 of this chapter;

(b) there is probable cause for belief that particular communications concerning that offense will be obtained through such interception;

(c) normal investigative procedures have been tried and have failed or reasonably appear to be unlikely to succeed if tried or to be too dangerous;

(d) except as provided in subsection (11), there is probable cause for belief that the facilities from which, or the place where, the wire, oral, or electronic communications are to be intercepted are being used, or are about to be used, in connection with the commission of such offense, or are leased to, listed in the name of, or commonly used by such person.

(4) Each order authorizing or approving the interception of any wire, oral, or electronic communication under this chapter shall specify—

(a) the identity of the person, if known, whose communications are to be intercepted;

(b) the nature and location of the communications facilities as to which, or the place where, authority to intercept is granted;

(c) a particular description of the type of communication sought to be intercepted, and a statement of the particular offense to which it relates;

(d) the identity of the agency authorized to intercept the communications, and of the person authorizing the application; and

(e) the period of time during which such interception is authorized, including a statement as to whether or not the interception shall automatically terminate when the described communication has been first obtained.

An order authorizing the interception of a wire, oral, or electronic communication under this chapter shall, upon request of the applicant, direct that a provider of wire or electronic communication service, landlord, custodian or other person shall furnish the applicant forthwith all information, facilities, and technical assistance necessary to accomplish the interception unobtrusively and with a minimum of interference with the services that such service provider, landlord, custodian, or person is according the person whose communications are to be intercepted. Any provider of wire or electronic communication service, landlord, custodian or other person furnishing such facilities or technical assistance shall be compensated therefor by the applicant for reasonable expenses incurred in providing such facilities or assistance. Pursuant to section 2522 of this chapter, an order may also be issued to enforce the assistance capability and capacity requirements under the Communications Assistance for Law Enforcement Act.

(5) No order entered under this section may authorize or approve the interception of any wire, oral, or electronic communication for any period longer than is necessary to achieve the objective of the authorization, nor in any event longer than thirty days. Such thirty-day period begins on the earlier of the day on which the investigative or law enforcement officer first begins to conduct an interception under the order or ten days after the order is entered. Extensions of an order may be granted, but only upon application for an extension made in accordance with subsection (1) of this section and the court making the findings required by subsection (3) of this section. The period of extension shall be no longer than the authorizing judge deems necessary to achieve the purposes for which it was granted and in no event for longer than thirty days. Every order and extension thereof shall contain a provision that the authorization to intercept shall be executed as soon as practicable, shall be conducted in such a way as to minimize the interception of communications not otherwise subject to interception under this chapter, and must terminate upon attainment of the authorized objective, or in any event in thirty days. In the event the intercepted communication is in a code or foreign language, and an expert in that foreign language or code is not reasonably available during the interception period, minimization may be accomplished as soon as practicable after such interception. An interception under this chapter may be conducted in whole or in part by Government personnel, or by an individual operating under a contract with the Government, acting under the supervision of an investigative or law enforcement officer authorized to conduct the interception.

(6) Whenever an order authorizing interception is entered pursuant to this chapter, the order may require reports to be made to the judge who issued the order showing what progress has been made toward achievement of the authorized objective and the need for continued interception. Such reports shall be made at such intervals as the judge may require.

(7) Notwithstanding any other provision of this chapter, any investigative or law enforcement officer, specially designated by the Attorney General, the Deputy Attorney General, the Associate Attorney General, or by the principal prosecuting attorney of any State or subdivision thereof acting pursuant to a statute of that State, who reasonably determines that—

> **(a)** an emergency situation exists that involves—
>
>> **(i)** immediate danger of death or serious physical injury to any person,
>>
>> **(ii)** conspiratorial activities threatening the national security interest, or
>>
>> **(iii)** conspiratorial activities characteristic of organized crime,
>
> that requires a wire, oral, or electronic communication to be intercepted before an order authorizing such interception can, with due diligence, be obtained, and
>
> **(b)** there are grounds upon which an order could be entered under this chapter to authorize such interception,

may intercept such wire, oral, or electronic communication if an application for an order approving the interception is made in accordance with this section within forty-eight hours after the interception has occurred, or begins to occur. In the absence of an order, such interception shall immediately terminate when the communication sought is obtained or when the application for the order is denied, whichever is earlier. In the event such application for approval is denied, or in any other case where the interception is terminated without an order having been issued, the contents of any wire, oral, or electronic communication intercepted shall be treated as having been obtained in violation of this chapter, and an inventory shall be served as provided for in subsection (d) of this section on the person named in the application.

(8)(a) The contents of any wire, oral, or electronic communication intercepted by any means authorized by this chapter shall, if possible, be recorded on tape or wire or other comparable device. The recording of the contents of any wire, oral, or electronic communication under this subsection shall be done in such a way as will protect the recording from editing or other alterations. Immediately upon the expiration of the period of the order, or extensions thereof, such recordings shall be made available to the judge issuing such order and sealed under his directions. Custody of the recordings shall be wherever the judge orders. They shall not be destroyed except upon an order of the issuing or denying judge and in any event shall be kept for ten years. Duplicate recordings may be made for use or disclosure pursuant to the provisions of subsections (1) and (2) of section 2517 of this chapter for investigations. The presence of the seal provided for by this subsection, or a satisfactory explanation for the absence thereof, shall be a prerequisite for the use or disclosure of the contents of any wire, oral, or electronic communication or evidence derived therefrom under subsection (3) of section 2517.

(b) Applications made and orders granted under this chapter shall be sealed by the judge. Custody of the applications and orders shall be wherever the judge directs. Such applications and orders shall be disclosed only upon a showing of good cause before a judge of competent jurisdiction and shall not be destroyed except on order of the issuing or denying judge, and in any event shall be kept for ten years.

(c) Any violation of the provisions of this subsection may be punished as contempt of the issuing or denying judge.

(d) Within a reasonable time but not later than ninety days after the filing of an application for an order of approval under section 2518(7)(b) which is denied or the termination of the period of an order or extensions thereof, the issuing or denying judge shall cause to be served, on the persons named in the order or the application, and such other parties to intercepted communications as the judge may determine in his discretion that is in the interest of justice, an inventory which shall include notice of—

    (1) the fact of the entry of the order or the application;

    (2) the date of the entry and the period of authorized, approved or disapproved interception, or the denial of the application; and

    (3) the fact that during the period wire, oral, or electronic communications were or were not intercepted.

The judge, upon the filing of a motion, may in his discretion make available to such person or his counsel for inspection such portions of the intercepted communications, applications and orders as the judge determines to be in the interest of justice. On an ex parte showing of good cause to a judge of competent jurisdiction the serving of the inventory required by this subsection may be postponed.

(9) The contents of any wire, oral, or electronic communication intercepted pursuant to this chapter or evidence derived therefrom shall not be received in evidence or otherwise disclosed in any trial, hearing, or other proceeding in a Federal or State court unless each party, not less than ten days before the trial, hearing, or proceeding, has been furnished with a copy of the court order, and accompanying application, under which the interception was authorized or approved. This ten-day period may be waived by the judge if he finds that it was not possible to furnish the party with the above information ten days before the trial, hearing, or proceeding and that the party will not be prejudiced by the delay in receiving such information.

(10)(a) Any aggrieved person in any trial, hearing, or proceeding in or before any court, department, officer, agency, regulatory body, or other authority of the United States, a State, or a political subdivision thereof, may move to suppress the contents of any wire or oral communication intercepted pursuant to this chapter, or evidence derived therefrom, on the grounds that—

> **(i)** the communication was unlawfully intercepted;
>
> **(ii)** the order of authorization or approval under which it was intercepted is insufficient on its face; or
>
> **(iii)** the interception was not made in conformity with the order of authorization or approval.

Such motion shall be made before the trial, hearing, or proceeding unless there was no opportunity to make such motion or the person was not aware of the grounds of the motion. If the motion is granted, the contents of the intercepted wire or oral communication, or evidence derived therefrom, shall be treated as having been obtained in violation of this chapter. The judge, upon the filing of such motion by the aggrieved person, may in his discretion make available to the aggrieved person or his counsel for inspection such portions of the intercepted communication or evidence derived therefrom as the judge determines to be in the interests of justice.

(b) In addition to any other right to appeal, the United States shall have the right to appeal from an order granting a motion to suppress made under paragraph (a) of this subsection, or the denial of an application for an order of approval, if the United States attorney shall certify to the judge or other official granting such motion or denying such application that the appeal is not taken for purposes of delay. Such appeal shall be taken within thirty days after the date the order was entered and shall be diligently prosecuted.

(c) The remedies and sanctions described in this chapter with respect to the interception of electronic communications are the only judicial remedies and sanctions for nonconstitutional violations of this chapter involving such communications.

(11) The requirements of subsections (1)(b)(ii) and (3)(d) of this section relating to the specification of the facilities from which, or the place where, the communication is to be intercepted do not apply if—

(a) in the case of an application with respect to the interception of an oral communication—

(i) the application is by a Federal investigative or law enforcement officer and is approved by the Attorney General, the Deputy Attorney General, the Associate Attorney General, an Assistant Attorney General, or an acting Assistant Attorney General;

(ii) the application contains a full and complete statement as to why such specification is not practical and identifies the person committing the offense and whose communications are to be intercepted; and

(iii) the judge finds that such specification is not practical; and

(b) in the case of an application with respect to a wire or electronic communication—

(i) the application is by a Federal investigative or law enforcement officer and is approved by the Attorney General, the Deputy Attorney General, the Associate Attorney General, an Assistant Attorney General, or an acting Assistant Attorney General;

(ii) the application identifies the person believed to be committing the offense and whose communications are to be intercepted and the applicant makes a showing that there is probable cause to believe that the person's actions could have the effect of thwarting interception from a specified facility;

(iii) the judge finds that such showing has been adequately made; and

(iv) the order authorizing or approving the interception is limited to interception only for such time as it is reasonable to presume that the person identified in the application is or was reasonably proximate to the instrument through which such communication will be or was transmitted.

(12) An interception of a communication under an order with respect to which the requirements of subsections (1)(b)(ii) and (3)(d) of this section do not apply by reason of subsection (11)(a) shall not begin until the place where the communication is to be intercepted is ascertained by the person implementing the interception order. A provider of wire or electronic communications service that has received an order as provided for in subsection (11)(b) may move the court to modify or quash the order on the ground that its assistance with respect to the interception cannot be performed in a timely or reasonable fashion. The court, upon notice to the government, shall decide such a motion expeditiously.

18 U.S.C. § 2519. REPORTS CONCERNING INTERCEPTED WIRE, ORAL, OR ELECTRONIC COMMUNICATIONS

(1) Within thirty days after the expiration of an order (or each extension thereof) entered under section 2518, or the denial of an order approving an interception, the issuing or denying judge shall report to the Administrative Office of the United States Courts—

(a) the fact that an order or extension was applied for;

(b) the kind of order or extension applied for (including whether or not the order was an order with respect to which the requirements of sections 2518(1)(b)(ii) and 2518(3)(d) of this title did not apply by reason of section 2518(11) of this title);

(c) the fact that the order or extension was granted as applied for, was modified, or was denied;

(d) the period of interceptions authorized by the order, and the number and duration of any extensions of the order;

(e) the offense specified in the order or application, or extension of an order;

(f) the identity of the applying investigative or law enforcement officer and agency making the application and the person authorizing the application; and

(g) the nature of the facilities from which or the place where communications were to be intercepted.

(2) In January of each year the Attorney General, an Assistant Attorney General specially designated by the Attorney General, or the principal prosecuting attorney of a State, or the principal prosecuting attorney for any political subdivision of a State, shall report to the Administrative Office of the United States Courts—

(a) the information required by paragraphs (a) through (g) of subsection (1) of this section with respect to each application for an order or extension made during the preceding calendar year;

(b) a general description of the interceptions made under such order or extension, including (i) the approximate nature and frequency of incriminating communications intercepted, (ii) the approximate nature and frequency of other communications intercepted, (iii) the approximate number of persons whose communications were intercepted, (iv) the number of orders in which encryption was encountered and whether such encryption prevented law enforcement from obtaining the plain text of communications intercepted pursuant to such order, and (v) the approximate nature, amount, and cost of the manpower and other resources used in the interceptions;

(c) the number of arrests resulting from interceptions made under such order or extension, and the offenses for which arrests were made;

(d) the number of trials resulting from such interceptions;

(e) the number of motions to suppress made with respect to such interceptions, and the number granted or denied;

(f) the number of convictions resulting from such interceptions and the offenses for which the convictions were obtained and a general assessment of the importance of the interceptions; and

(g) the information required by paragraphs (b) through (f) of this subsection with respect to orders or extensions obtained in a preceding calendar year.

(3) In April of each year the Director of the Administrative Office of the United States Courts shall transmit to the Congress a full and complete report concerning the number of applications for orders authorizing or approving the interception of wire, oral, or electronic communications pursuant to this chapter and the number of orders and extensions granted or denied pursuant to this chapter during the preceding calendar year. Such report shall include a summary and analysis of the data required to be filed with the Administrative Office by subsections (1) and (2) of this section. The Director of the Administrative Office of the United States Courts is authorized to issue binding regulations dealing with the content and form of the reports required to be filed by subsections (1) and (2) of this section.

18 U.S.C. § 2520. RECOVERY OF CIVIL DAMAGES AUTHORIZED

(a) In general. Except as provided in section 2511(2)(a)(ii), any person whose wire, oral, or electronic communication is intercepted, disclosed, or intentionally used in violation of this chapter may in a civil action recover from the person or entity, other than the United States, which engaged in that violation such relief as may be appropriate.

(b) Relief. In an action under this section, appropriate relief includes—

(1) such preliminary and other equitable or declaratory relief as may be appropriate;

(2) damages under subsection (c) and punitive damages in appropriate cases; and

(3) a reasonable attorney's fee and other litigation costs reasonably incurred.

(c) Computation of damages.

(1) In an action under this section, if the conduct in violation of this chapter is the private viewing of a private satellite video communication that is not scrambled or encrypted or if the communication is a radio communication that is transmitted on frequencies allocated under subpart D of part 74 of the rules of the Federal Communications Commission that is not scrambled or encrypted and the conduct is not for a tortious or illegal purpose or for purposes of direct or indirect commercial advantage or private commercial gain, then the court shall assess damages as follows:

(A) If the person who engaged in that conduct has not previously been enjoined under section 2511(5) and has not been found liable in a prior civil action under this section, the court shall assess the greater of the sum of actual damages suffered by the plaintiff, or statutory damages of not less than $50 and not more than $500.

(B) If, on one prior occasion, the person who engaged in that conduct has been enjoined under section 2511(5) or has been found liable in a civil action under this section, the court shall assess the greater of the sum of actual damages suffered by the plaintiff, or statutory damages of not less than $100 and not more than $1000.

(2) In any other action under this section, the court may assess as damages whichever is the greater of—

(A) the sum of the actual damages suffered by the plaintiff and any profits made by the violator as a result of the violation; or

(B) statutory damages of whichever is the greater of $100 a day for each day of violation or $10,000.

(d) Defense. A good faith reliance on—

(1) a court warrant or order, a grand jury subpoena, a legislative authorization, or a statutory authorization;

(2) a request of an investigative or law enforcement officer under section 2518(7) of this title; or

(3) a good faith determination that section 2511(3), 2511(2)(i), or 2511(2)(j) of this title permitted the conduct complained of;

is a complete defense against any civil or criminal action brought under this chapter or any other law.

(e) Limitation. A civil action under this section may not be commenced later than two years after the date upon which the claimant first has a reasonable opportunity to discover the violation.

(f) Administrative discipline. If a court or appropriate department or agency determines that the United States or any of its departments or agencies has violated any provision of this chapter, and the court or appropriate department or agency finds that the circumstances surrounding the violation raise serious questions about whether or not an officer or employee of the United States acted willfully or intentionally with respect to the violation, the department or agency shall, upon receipt of a true and correct copy of the decision and findings of the court or appropriate department or agency promptly initiate a proceeding to determine whether disciplinary action against the officer or employee is warranted. If the head of the department or agency involved determines that disciplinary action is not warranted, he or she shall notify the Inspector General with jurisdiction over the department or agency concerned and shall provide the Inspector General with the reasons for such determination.

(g) Improper disclosure is violation. Any willful disclosure or use by an investigative or law enforcement officer or governmental entity of information beyond the extent permitted by section 2517 is a violation of this chapter for purposes of section 2520(a).

18 U.S.C. § 2521. INJUNCTION AGAINST ILLEGAL INTERCEPTION

Whenever it shall appear that any person is engaged or is about to engage in any act which constitutes or will constitute a felony violation of this chapter, the Attorney General may initiate a civil action in a district court of the United States to enjoin such violation. The court shall proceed as soon as practicable to the hearing and determination of such an action, and may, at any time before final determination, enter such a restraining order or prohibition, or take such other action, as is warranted to prevent a continuing and substantial injury to the United States or to any person or class of persons for whose protection the action is brought. A proceeding under this section is governed by the Federal Rules of Civil Procedure, except that, if an indictment has been returned against the respondent, discovery is governed by the Federal Rules of Criminal Procedure.

18 U.S.C. § 2522. ENFORCEMENT OF THE COMMUNICATIONS ASSISTANCE FOR LAW ENFORCEMENT ACT

(a) Enforcement by court issuing surveillance order. If a court authorizing an interception under this chapter, a State statute, or the

Foreign Intelligence Surveillance Act of 1978 (50 U.S.C. 1801 et seq.) or authorizing use of a pen register or a trap and trace device under chapter 206 or a State statute finds that a telecommunications carrier has failed to comply with the requirements of the Communications Assistance for Law Enforcement Act, the court may, in accordance with section 108 of such Act, direct that the carrier comply forthwith and may direct that a provider of support services to the carrier or the manufacturer of the carrier's transmission or switching equipment furnish forthwith modifications necessary for the carrier to comply.

(b) Enforcement upon application by Attorney General. The Attorney General may, in a civil action in the appropriate United States district court, obtain an order, in accordance with section 108 of the Communications Assistance for Law Enforcement Act, directing that a telecommunications carrier, a manufacturer of telecommunications transmission or switching equipment, or a provider of telecommunications support services comply with such Act.

(c) Civil penalty.—

(1) In general. A court issuing an order under this section against a telecommunications carrier, a manufacturer of telecommunications transmission or switching equipment, or a provider of telecommunications support services may impose a civil penalty of up to $10,000 per day for each day in violation after the issuance of the order or after such future date as the court may specify.

(2) Considerations. In determining whether to impose a civil penalty and in determining its amount, the court shall take into account—

(A) the nature, circumstances, and extent of the violation;

(B) the violator's ability to pay, the violator's good faith efforts to comply in a timely manner, any effect on the violator's ability to continue to do business, the degree of culpability, and the length of any delay in undertaking efforts to comply; and

(C) such other matters as justice may require.

(d) Definitions. As used in this section, the terms defined in section 102 of the Communications Assistance for Law Enforcement Act have the meanings provided, respectively, in such section.

18 U.S.C. § 2523. EXECUTIVE AGREEMENTS ON ACCESS TO DATA BY FOREIGN GOVERNMENTS

(a) Definitions. In this section—

(1) the term "lawfully admitted for permanent residence" has the meaning given the term in section 101(a) of the Immigration and Nationality Act (8 U.S.C. 1101(a)); and

(2) the term "United States person" means a citizen or national of the United States, an alien lawfully admitted for permanent residence, an unincorporated association a substantial number of members of which are citizens of the United States or aliens lawfully admitted for permanent residence, or a corporation that is incorporated in the United States.

(b) **Executive agreement requirements.**—For purposes of this chapter, chapter 121, and chapter 206, an executive agreement governing access by a foreign government to data subject to this chapter, chapter 121, or chapter 206 shall be considered to satisfy the requirements of this section if the Attorney General, with the concurrence of the Secretary of State, determines, and submits a written certification of such determination to Congress, including a written certification and explanation of each consideration in paragraphs (1), (2), (3), and (4), that—

(1) the domestic law of the foreign government, including the implementation of that law, affords robust substantive and procedural protections for privacy and civil liberties in light of the data collection and activities of the foreign government that will be subject to the agreement, if—

(A) such a determination under this section takes into account, as appropriate, credible information and expert input; and

(B) the factors to be met in making such a determination include whether the foreign government—

(i) has adequate substantive and procedural laws on cybercrime and electronic evidence, as demonstrated by being a party to the Convention on Cybercrime, done at Budapest November 23, 2001, and entered into force January 7, 2004, or through domestic laws that are consistent with definitions and the requirements set forth in chapters I and II of that Convention;

(ii) demonstrates respect for the rule of law and principles of nondiscrimination;

(iii) adheres to applicable international human rights obligations and commitments or demonstrates respect for international universal human rights, including—

(I) protection from arbitrary and unlawful interference with privacy;

(II) fair trial rights;

(III) freedom of expression, association, and peaceful assembly;

(IV) prohibitions on arbitrary arrest and detention; and

(V) prohibitions against torture and cruel, inhuman, or degrading treatment or punishment;

(iv) has clear legal mandates and procedures governing those entities of the foreign government that are authorized to seek data under the executive agreement, including procedures through which those authorities collect, retain, use, and share data, and effective oversight of these activities;

(v) has sufficient mechanisms to provide accountability and appropriate transparency regarding the collection and use of electronic data by the foreign government; and

(vi) demonstrates a commitment to promote and protect the global free flow of information and the open, distributed, and interconnected nature of the Internet;

(2) the foreign government has adopted appropriate procedures to minimize the acquisition, retention, and dissemination of information concerning United States persons subject to the agreement;

(3) the terms of the agreement shall not create any obligation that providers be capable of decrypting data or limitation that prevents providers from decrypting data; and

(4) the agreement requires that, with respect to any order that is subject to the agreement—

(A) the foreign government may not intentionally target a United States person or a person located in the United States, and shall adopt targeting procedures designed to meet this requirement;

(B) the foreign government may not target a non-United States person located outside the United States if the purpose is to obtain information concerning a United States person or a person located in the United States;

(C) the foreign government may not issue an order at the request of or to obtain information to provide to the United States Government or a third-party government, nor shall the foreign government be required to share any information produced with the United States Government or a third-party government;

(D) an order issued by the foreign government—

(i) shall be for the purpose of obtaining information relating to the prevention, detection, investigation, or prosecution of serious crime, including terrorism;

(ii) shall identify a specific person, account, address, or personal device, or any other specific identifier as the object of the order;

(iii) shall be in compliance with the domestic law of that country, and any obligation for a provider of an electronic communications service or a remote computing service to produce data shall derive solely from that law;

(iv) shall be based on requirements for a reasonable justification based on articulable and credible facts, particularity, legality, and severity regarding the conduct under investigation;

(v) shall be subject to review or oversight by a court, judge, magistrate, or other independent authority prior to, or in proceedings regarding, enforcement of the order; and

(vi) in the case of an order for the interception of wire or electronic communications, and any extensions thereof, shall require that the interception order—

(I) be for a fixed, limited duration; and

(II) may not last longer than is reasonably necessary to accomplish the approved purposes of the order; and

(III) be issued only if the same information could not reasonably be obtained by another less intrusive method;

(E) an order issued by the foreign government may not be used to infringe freedom of speech;

(F) the foreign government shall promptly review material collected pursuant to the agreement and store any unreviewed communications on a secure system accessible only to those persons trained in applicable procedures;

(G) the foreign government shall, using procedures that, to the maximum extent possible, meet the definition of minimization procedures in section 101 of the Foreign Intelligence Surveillance Act of 1978 (50 U.S.C. 1801), segregate, seal, or delete, and not disseminate material found not to be information that is, or is necessary to understand or assess the importance of information that is, relevant to the prevention, detection, investigation, or prosecution of serious crime, including terrorism, or necessary to protect against a threat of death or serious bodily harm to any person;

(H) the foreign government may not disseminate the content of a communication of a United States person to United States authorities unless the communication may be disseminated pursuant to subparagraph (G) and relates to significant harm, or the threat thereof, to the United States or United States persons, including crimes involving national security such as terrorism, significant violent crime, child exploitation, transnational organized crime, or significant financial fraud;

(I) the foreign government shall afford reciprocal rights of data access, to include, where applicable, removing restrictions on communications service providers, including providers subject to United States jurisdiction, and thereby allow them to respond to valid legal process sought by a governmental entity (as defined in section 2711) if foreign law would otherwise prohibit communications-service providers from disclosing the data;

(J) the foreign government shall agree to periodic review of compliance by the foreign government with the terms of the agreement to be conducted by the United States Government; and

(K) the United States Government shall reserve the right to render the agreement inapplicable as to any order for which the United States Government concludes the agreement may not properly be invoked.

(c) Limitation on judicial review.—A determination or certification made by the Attorney General under subsection (b) shall not be subject to judicial or administrative review.

(d) Effective date of certification.—

(1) Notice.—Not later than 7 days after the date on which the Attorney General certifies an executive agreement under subsection (b), the Attorney General shall provide notice of the determination under subsection (b) and a copy of the executive agreement to Congress, including—

(A) the Committee on the Judiciary and the Committee on Foreign Relations of the Senate; and

(B) the Committee on the Judiciary and the Committee on Foreign Affairs of the House of Representatives.

(2) Entry into force.—An executive agreement that is determined and certified by the Attorney General to satisfy the requirements of this section shall enter into force not earlier than the date that is 180 days after the date on which notice is provided under paragraph (1), unless Congress enacts a joint resolution of disapproval in accordance with paragraph (4).

(3) Requests for information.—Upon request by the Chairman or Ranking Member of a congressional committee described in paragraph (1), the head of an agency shall promptly furnish a summary of factors considered in determining that the foreign government satisfies the requirements of this section.

(4) Congressional review.—

(A) Joint resolution defined.—In this paragraph, the term "joint resolution" means only a joint resolution—

(i) introduced during the 180-day period described in paragraph (2);

(ii) which does not have a preamble;

(iii) the title of which is as follows: "Joint resolution disapproving the executive agreement signed by the United States and ___.", the blank space being appropriately filled in; and

(iv) the matter after the resolving clause of which is as follows: "That Congress disapproves the executive agreement governing access by ____ to certain electronic data as submitted by the Attorney General on ____", the blank spaces being appropriately filled in.

(B) Joint resolution enacted.—Notwithstanding any other provision of this section, if not later than 180 days after the date on which notice is provided to Congress under paragraph (1), there is enacted into law a joint resolution disapproving of an executive agreement under this section, the executive agreement shall not enter into force.

(C) Introduction.—During the 180-day period described in subparagraph (B), a joint resolution of disapproval may be introduced—

(i) in the House of Representatives, by the majority leader or the minority leader; and

(ii) in the Senate, by the majority leader (or the majority leader's designee) or the minority leader (or the minority leader's designee).

(5) Floor consideration in House of Representatives.—If a committee of the House of Representatives to which a joint resolution of disapproval has been referred has not reported the joint resolution within 120 days after the date of referral, that committee shall be discharged from further consideration of the joint resolution.

(6) Consideration in the Senate.—

(A) Committee referral.—A joint resolution of disapproval introduced in the Senate shall be referred jointly—

(i) to the Committee on the Judiciary; and

(ii) to the Committee on Foreign Relations.

(B) Reporting and discharge.—If a committee to which a joint resolution of disapproval was referred has not reported the joint resolution within 120 days after the date of referral of the joint resolution, that committee shall be discharged from further consideration of the joint resolution and the joint resolution shall be placed on the appropriate calendar.

(C) Proceeding to consideration.—It is in order at any time after both the Committee on the Judiciary and the Committee on Foreign Relations report a joint resolution of disapproval to the Senate or have been discharged from consideration of such a joint resolution (even though a previous motion to the same effect has been disagreed to) to move to proceed to the consideration of the joint resolution, and all points of order against the joint resolution (and against consideration of the joint resolution) are waived. The motion is not debatable or subject to a motion to postpone. A motion to reconsider the vote by which the motion is agreed to or disagreed to shall not be in order.

(D) Consideration in the Senate.—In the Senate, consideration of the joint resolution, and on all debatable motions and appeals in connection therewith, shall be limited to not more than 10 hours, which shall be divided equally between those favoring and those opposing the joint resolution. A motion further to limit debate is in order and not debatable. An amendment to, or a motion to postpone, or a motion to proceed to the consideration of other business, or a motion to recommit the joint resolution is not in order.

(E) Consideration of veto messages.—Debate in the Senate of any veto message with respect to a joint resolution of disapproval, including all debatable motions and appeals in connection with the joint resolution, shall be limited to 10 hours, to be equally divided between, and controlled by, the majority leader and the minority leader or their designees.

(7) Rules relating to Senate and House of Representatives.—

(A) Treatment of Senate Joint Resolution in House.— In the House of Representatives, the following procedures shall apply to a joint resolution of disapproval received from the Senate (unless the House has already passed a joint resolution relating to the same proposed action):

(i) The joint resolution shall be referred to the appropriate committees.

(ii) If a committee to which a joint resolution has been referred has not reported the joint resolution within 7 days after the date of referral, that committee shall be discharged from further consideration of the joint resolution.

(iii) Beginning on the third legislative day after each committee to which a joint resolution has been referred reports the joint resolution to the House or has been discharged from further consideration thereof, it shall be in order to move to proceed to consider the joint resolution in the House. All points of order against the motion are waived. Such a motion shall not be in order after the House has disposed of a motion to proceed on the joint resolution. The previous question shall be considered as ordered on the motion to its adoption without intervening motion. The motion shall not be debatable. A motion to reconsider the vote by which the motion is disposed of shall not be in order.

(iv) The joint resolution shall be considered as read. All points of order against the joint resolution and against its consideration are waived. The previous question shall be considered as ordered on the joint resolution to final passage without intervening motion except 2 hours of debate equally divided and controlled by the sponsor of the joint resolution (or a designee) and an opponent. A motion to reconsider the vote on passage of the joint resolution shall not be in order.

(B) Treatment of House Joint Resolution in Senate.—

(i) If, before the passage by the Senate of a joint resolution of disapproval, the Senate receives an identical joint resolution from the House of Representatives, the following procedures shall apply:

(I) That joint resolution shall not be referred to a committee.

(II) With respect to that joint resolution—

(aa) the procedure in the Senate shall be the same as if no joint resolution had been received from the House of Representatives; but

(bb) the vote on passage shall be on the joint resolution from the House of Representatives.

(ii) If, following passage of a joint resolution of disapproval in the Senate, the Senate receives an identical joint resolution from the House of Representatives, that joint resolution shall be placed on the appropriate Senate calendar.

(iii) If a joint resolution of disapproval is received from the House, and no companion joint resolution has been introduced in the Senate, the Senate procedures under this subsection shall apply to the House joint resolution.

(C) Application to revenue measures.—The provisions of this paragraph shall not apply in the House of Representatives to a joint resolution of disapproval that is a revenue measure.

(8) Rules of House of Representatives and Senate.—This subsection is enacted by Congress—

(A) as an exercise of the rulemaking power of the Senate and the House of Representatives, respectively, and as such is deemed a part of the rules of each House, respectively, and supersedes other rules only to the extent that it is inconsistent with such rules; and

(B) with full recognition of the constitutional right of either House to change the rules (so far as relating to the procedure of that House) at any time, in the same manner, and to the same extent as in the case of any other rule of that House.

(e) Renewal of determination.—

(1) In general.—The Attorney General, with the concurrence of the Secretary of State, shall review and may renew a determination under subsection (b) every 5 years.

(2) Report.—Upon renewing a determination under subsection (b), the Attorney General shall file a report with the Committee on the Judiciary and the Committee on Foreign Relations of the Senate and the Committee on the Judiciary and the Committee on Foreign Affairs of the House of Representatives describing—

(A) the reasons for the renewal;

(B) any substantive changes to the agreement or to the relevant laws or procedures of the foreign government since the original determination or, in the case of a second or subsequent renewal, since the last renewal; and

(C) how the agreement has been implemented and what problems or controversies, if any, have arisen as a result of the agreement or its implementation.

(3) Nonrenewal.—If a determination is not renewed under paragraph (1), the agreement shall no longer be considered to satisfy the requirements of this section.

(f) Revisions to agreement.—A revision to an agreement under this section shall be treated as a new agreement for purposes of this section and shall be subject to the certification requirement under subsection (b), and to the procedures under subsection (d), except that for purposes of a revision to an agreement—

(1) the applicable time period under paragraphs (2), (4)(A)(i), (4)(B), and (4)(C) of subsection (d) shall be 90 days after the date notice is provided under subsection (d)(1); and

(2) the applicable time period under paragraphs (5) and (6)(B) of subsection (d) shall be 60 days after the date notice is provided under subsection (d)(1).

(g) Publication.—Any determination or certification under subsection (b) regarding an executive agreement under this section, including any termination or renewal of such an agreement, shall be published in the Federal Register as soon as is reasonably practicable.

(h) Minimization procedures.—A United States authority that receives the content of a communication described in subsection (b)(4)(H) from a foreign government in accordance with an executive agreement under this section shall use procedures that, to the maximum extent possible, meet the definition of minimization procedures in section 101 of the Foreign Intelligence Surveillance Act of 1978 (50 U.S.C. 1801) to appropriately protect nonpublicly available information concerning United States persons.

18 U.S.C. § 2701. UNLAWFUL ACCESS TO STORED COMMUNICATIONS

(a) Offense. Except as provided in subsection (c) of this section whoever—

(1) intentionally accesses without authorization a facility through which an electronic communication service is provided; or

(2) intentionally exceeds an authorization to access that facility;

and thereby obtains, alters, or prevents authorized access to a wire or electronic communication while it is in electronic storage in such system shall be punished as provided in subsection (b) of this section.

(b) Punishment. The punishment for an offense under subsection (a) of this section is—

(1) if the offense is committed for purposes of commercial advantage, malicious destruction or damage, or private commercial gain, or in furtherance of any criminal or tortious act in violation of the Constitution or laws of the United States or any State—

(A) a fine under this title or imprisonment for not more than 5 years, or both, in the case of a first offense under this subparagraph; and

(B) a fine under this title or imprisonment for not more than 10 years, or both, for any subsequent offense under this subparagraph; and

(2) in any other case—

(A) a fine under this title or imprisonment for not more than 1 year or both, in the case of a first offense under this paragraph; and

(B) a fine under this title or imprisonment for not more than 5 years, or both, in the case of an offense under this subparagraph that occurs after a conviction of another offense under this section.

(c) Exceptions. Subsection (a) of this section does not apply with respect to conduct authorized—

(1) by the person or entity providing a wire or electronic communications service;

(2) by a user of that service with respect to a communication of or intended for that user; or

(3) in section 2703, 2704 or 2518 of this title.

18 U.S.C. § 2702. VOLUNTARY DISCLOSURE OF CUSTOMER COMMUNICATIONS OR RECORDS

(a) Prohibitions. Except as provided in subsection (b) or (c)—

(1) a person or entity providing an electronic communication service to the public shall not knowingly divulge to any person or entity the contents of a communication while in electronic storage by that service; and

(2) a person or entity providing remote computing service to the public shall not knowingly divulge to any person or entity the contents of any communication which is carried or maintained on that service—

(A) on behalf of, and received by means of electronic transmission from (or created by means of computer processing of communications received by means of electronic transmission from), a subscriber or customer of such service;

(B) solely for the purpose of providing storage or computer processing services to such subscriber or customer, if the provider is not authorized to access the contents of any such communications for purposes of providing any services other than storage or computer processing; and

(3) a provider of remote computing service or electronic communication service to the public shall not knowingly divulge a record or other information pertaining to a subscriber to or customer of such service (not including the contents of communications covered by paragraph (1) or (2)) to any governmental entity.

(b) Exceptions for disclosure of communications. A provider described in subsection (a) may divulge the contents of a communication—

(1) to an addressee or intended recipient of such communication or an agent of such addressee or intended recipient;

(2) as otherwise authorized in section 2517, 2511(2)(a), or 2703 of this title;

(3) with the lawful consent of the originator or an addressee or intended recipient of such communication, or the subscriber in the case of remote computing service;

(4) to a person employed or authorized or whose facilities are used to forward such communication to its destination;

(5) as may be necessarily incident to the rendition of the service or to the protection of the rights or property of the provider of that service;

(6) to the National Center for Missing and Exploited Children, in connection with a report submitted thereto under section 2258A;

(7) to a law enforcement agency—

(A) if the contents—

(i) were inadvertently obtained by the service provider; and

(ii) appear to pertain to the commission of a crime; or

(8) to a governmental entity, if the provider, in good faith, believes that an emergency involving danger of death or serious physical injury to any person requires disclosure without delay of communications relating to the emergency;

(9) to a foreign government pursuant to an order from a foreign government that is subject to an executive agreement that the

Attorney General has determined and certified to Congress satisfies section 2523.

(c) Exceptions for disclosure of customer records. A provider described in subsection (a) may divulge a record or other information pertaining to a subscriber to or customer of such service (not including the contents of communications covered by subsection (a)(1) or (a)(2))—

(1) as otherwise authorized in section 2703;

(2) with the lawful consent of the customer or subscriber;

(3) as may be necessarily incident to the rendition of the service or to the protection of the rights or property of the provider of that service;

(4) to a governmental entity, if the provider, in good faith, believes that an emergency involving danger of death or serious physical injury to any person requires disclosure without delay of information relating to the emergency;

(5) to the National Center for Missing and Exploited Children, in connection with a report submitted thereto under section 2258A;

(6) to any person other than a governmental entity;

(7) to a foreign government pursuant to an order from a foreign government that is subject to an executive agreement that the Attorney General has determined and certified to Congress satisfies section 2523.

(d) Reporting of emergency disclosures. On an annual basis, the Attorney General shall submit to the Committee on the Judiciary of the House of Representatives and the Committee on the Judiciary of the Senate a report containing—

(1) the number of accounts from which the Department of Justice has received voluntary disclosures under subsection (b)(8); and

(2) a summary of the basis for disclosure in those instances where—

(A) voluntary disclosures under subsection (b)(8) were made to the Department of Justice; and

(B) the investigation pertaining to those disclosures was closed without the filing of criminal charges.

18 U.S.C. § 2703. REQUIRED DISCLOSURE OF CUSTOMER COMMUNICATIONS OR RECORDS

(a) Contents of wire or electronic communications in electronic storage. A governmental entity may require the disclosure by a provider of electronic communication service of the contents of a wire or electronic communication, that is in electronic storage in an electronic communications system for one hundred and eighty days or less, only pursuant to a warrant issued using the procedures described in the Federal Rules of Criminal Procedure (or, in the case of a State court, issued using State warrant procedures) by a court of competent jurisdiction. A governmental entity may require the disclosure by a provider of electronic communications services of the contents of a wire or electronic communication that has been in electronic storage in an electronic communications system for more than one hundred and eighty days by the means available under subsection (b) of this section.

(b) Contents of wire or electronic communications in a remote computing service.

(1) A governmental entity may require a provider of remote computing service to disclose the contents of any wire or electronic communication to which this paragraph is made applicable by paragraph (2) of this subsection—

(A) without required notice to the subscriber or customer, if the governmental entity obtains a warrant issued using the procedures described in the Federal Rules of Criminal Procedure (or, in the case of a State court, issued using State warrant procedures) by a court of competent jurisdiction; or

(B) with prior notice from the governmental entity to the subscriber or customer if the governmental entity—

(i) uses an administrative subpoena authorized by a Federal or State statute or a Federal or State grand jury or trial subpoena; or

(ii) obtains a court order for such disclosure under subsection (d) of this section;

except that delayed notice may be given pursuant to section 2705 of this title.

(2) Paragraph (1) is applicable with respect to any wire or electronic communication that is held or maintained on that service—

(A) on behalf of, and received by means of electronic transmission from (or created by means of computer processing of communications received by means of electronic transmission from), a subscriber or customer of such remote computing service; and

(B) solely for the purpose of providing storage or computer processing services to such subscriber or customer, if the provider is not authorized to access the contents of any such communications for purposes of providing any services other than storage or computer processing.

(c) Records concerning electronic communication service or remote computing service.

(1) A governmental entity may require a provider of electronic communication service or remote computing service to disclose a record or other information pertaining to a subscriber to or customer of such service (not including the contents of communications) only when the governmental entity—

(A) obtains a warrant issued using the procedures described in the Federal Rules of Criminal Procedure (or, in the case of a State court, issued using State warrant procedures) by a court of competent jurisdiction;

(B) obtains a court order for such disclosure under subsection (d) of this section;

(C) has the consent of the subscriber or customer to such disclosure;

(D) submits a formal written request relevant to a law enforcement investigation concerning telemarketing fraud for the name, address, and place of business of a subscriber or customer of such provider, which subscriber or customer is engaged in telemarketing (as such term is defined in section 2325 of this title); or

(E) seeks information under paragraph (2).

(2) A provider of electronic communication service or remote computing service shall disclose to a governmental entity the—

(A) name;

(B) address;

(C) local and long distance telephone connection records, or records of session times and durations;

(D) length of service (including start date) and types of service utilized;

(E) telephone or instrument number or other subscriber number or identity, including any temporarily assigned network address; and

(F) means and source of payment for such service (including any credit card or bank account number),

of a subscriber to or customer of such service when the governmental entity uses an administrative subpoena authorized by a Federal or

State statute or a Federal or State grand jury or trial subpoena or any means available under paragraph (1).

(3) A governmental entity receiving records or information under this subsection is not required to provide notice to a subscriber or customer.

(d) Requirements for court order. A court order for disclosure under subsection (b) or (c) may be issued by any court that is a court of competent jurisdiction and shall issue only if the governmental entity offers specific and articulable facts showing that there are reasonable grounds to believe that the contents of a wire or electronic communication, or the records or other information sought, are relevant and material to an ongoing criminal investigation. In the case of a State governmental authority, such a court order shall not issue if prohibited by the law of such State. A court issuing an order pursuant to this section, on a motion made promptly by the service provider, may quash or modify such order, if the information or records requested are unusually voluminous in nature or compliance with such order otherwise would cause an undue burden on such provider.

(e) No cause of action against a provider disclosing information under this chapter. No cause of action shall lie in any court against any provider of wire or electronic communication service, its officers, employees, agents, or other specified persons for providing information, facilities, or assistance in accordance with the terms of a court order, warrant, subpoena, statutory authorization, or certification under this chapter.

(f) Requirement to preserve evidence.

(1) In general. A provider of wire or electronic communication services or a remote computing service, upon the request of a governmental entity, shall take all necessary steps to preserve records and other evidence in its possession pending the issuance of a court order or other process.

(2) Period of retention. Records referred to in paragraph (1) shall be retained for a period of 90 days, which shall be extended for an additional 90-day period upon a renewed request by the governmental entity.

(g) Presence of officer not required. Notwithstanding section 3105 of this title, the presence of an officer shall not be required for service or execution of a search warrant issued in accordance with this chapter requiring disclosure by a provider of electronic communications service or remote computing service of the contents of communications or records or other information pertaining to a subscriber to or customer of such service.

(h) Comity analysis and disclosure of information regarding legal process seeking contents of wire or electronic communication.

(1) Definitions.—In this subsection—

(A) the term "qualifying foreign government" means a foreign government—

(i) with which the United States has an executive agreement that has entered into force under section 2523; and

(ii) the laws of which provide to electronic communication service providers and remote computing service providers substantive and procedural opportunities similar to those provided under paragraphs (2) and (5); and

(B) the term "United States person" has the meaning given the term in section 2523.

(2) Motions to quash or modify.—

(A) A provider of electronic communication service to the public or remote computing service, including a foreign electronic communication service or remote computing service, that is being required to disclose pursuant to legal process issued under this section the contents of a wire or electronic communication of a subscriber or customer, may file a motion to modify or quash the legal process where the provider reasonably believes—

(i) that the customer or subscriber is not a United States person and does not reside in the United States; and

(ii) that the required disclosure would create a material risk that the provider would violate the laws of a qualifying foreign government.

Such a motion shall be filed not later than 14 days after the date on which the provider was served with the legal process, absent agreement with the government or permission from the court to extend the deadline based on an application made within the 14 days. The right to move to quash is without prejudice to any other grounds to move to quash or defenses thereto, but it shall be the sole basis for moving to quash on the grounds of a conflict of law related to a qualifying foreign government.

(B) Upon receipt of a motion filed pursuant to subparagraph (A), the court shall afford the governmental entity that applied for or issued the legal process under this section the opportunity to respond. The court may modify or quash the legal process, as appropriate, only if the court finds that—

(i) the required disclosure would cause the provider to violate the laws of a qualifying foreign government;

(ii) based on the totality of the circumstances, the interests of justice dictate that the legal process should be modified or quashed; and

(iii) the customer or subscriber is not a United States person and does not reside in the United States.

(3) Comity analysis.—For purposes of making a determination under paragraph (2)(B)(ii), the court shall take into account, as appropriate—

(A) the interests of the United States, including the investigative interests of the governmental entity seeking to require the disclosure;

(B) the interests of the qualifying foreign government in preventing any prohibited disclosure;

(C) the likelihood, extent, and nature of penalties to the provider or any employees of the provider as a result of inconsistent legal requirements imposed on the provider;

(D) the location and nationality of the subscriber or customer whose communications are being sought, if known, and the nature and extent of the subscriber or customer's connection to the United States, or if the legal process has been sought on behalf of a foreign authority pursuant to section 3512, the nature and extent of the subscriber or customer's connection to the foreign authority's country;

(E) the nature and extent of the provider's ties to and presence in the United States;

(F) the importance to the investigation of the information required to be disclosed;

(G) the likelihood of timely and effective access to the information required to be disclosed through means that would cause less serious negative consequences; and

(H) if the legal process has been sought on behalf of a foreign authority pursuant to section 3512, the investigative interests of the foreign authority making the request for assistance.

(4) Disclosure obligations during pendency of challenge.—A service provider shall preserve, but not be obligated to produce, information sought during the pendency of a motion brought under this subsection, unless the court finds that immediate production is necessary to prevent an adverse result identified in section 2705(a)(2).

(5) Disclosure to qualifying foreign Government.

(A) It shall not constitute a violation of a protective order issued under section 2705 for a provider of electronic communication service to the public or remote computing service to disclose to the entity within a qualifying foreign government, designated in an executive agreement under section 2523, the fact of the existence of legal process issued under this section seeking the contents of a wire or electronic communication of a customer or subscriber who is a national or resident of the qualifying foreign government.

(B) Nothing in this paragraph shall be construed to modify or otherwise affect any other authority to make a motion to modify or quash a protective order issued under section 2705.

18 U.S.C. § 2704. BACKUP PRESERVATION

(a) Backup preservation.

(1) A governmental entity acting under section 2703(b)(2) may include in its subpoena or court order a requirement that the service provider to whom the request is directed create a backup copy of the contents of the electronic communications sought in order to preserve those communications. Without notifying the subscriber or customer of such subpoena or court order, such service provider shall create such backup copy as soon as practicable consistent with its regular business practices and shall confirm to the governmental entity that such backup copy has been made. Such backup copy shall be created within two business days after receipt by the service provider of the subpoena or court order.

(2) Notice to the subscriber or customer shall be made by the governmental entity within three days after receipt of such confirmation, unless such notice is delayed pursuant to section 2705(a).

(3) The service provider shall not destroy such backup copy until the later of—

(A) the delivery of the information; or

(B) the resolution of any proceedings (including appeals of any proceeding) concerning the government's subpoena or court order.

(4) The service provider shall release such backup copy to the requesting governmental entity no sooner than fourteen days after the governmental entity's notice to the subscriber or customer if such service provider—

    (A) has not received notice from the subscriber or customer that the subscriber or customer has challenged the governmental entity's request; and

    (B) has not initiated proceedings to challenge the request of the governmental entity.

  (5) A governmental entity may seek to require the creation of a backup copy under subsection (a)(1) of this section if in its sole discretion such entity determines that there is reason to believe that notification under section 2703 of this title of the existence of the subpoena or court order may result in destruction of or tampering with evidence. This determination is not subject to challenge by the subscriber or customer or service provider.

(b) Customer challenges.

  (1) Within fourteen days after notice by the governmental entity to the subscriber or customer under subsection (a)(2) of this section, such subscriber or customer may file a motion to quash such subpoena or vacate such court order, with copies served upon the governmental entity and with written notice of such challenge to the service provider. A motion to vacate a court order shall be filed in the court which issued such order. A motion to quash a subpoena shall be filed in the appropriate United States district court or State court. Such motion or application shall contain an affidavit or sworn statement—

    (A) stating that the applicant is a customer or subscriber to the service from which the contents of electronic communications maintained for him have been sought; and

    (B) stating the applicant's reasons for believing that the records sought are not relevant to a legitimate law enforcement inquiry or that there has not been substantial compliance with the provisions of this chapter in some other respect.

  (2) Service shall be made under this section upon a governmental entity by delivering or mailing by registered or certified mail a copy of the papers to the person, office, or department specified in the notice which the customer has received pursuant to this chapter. For the purposes of this section, the term "delivery" has the meaning given that term in the Federal Rules of Civil Procedure.

  (3) If the court finds that the customer has complied with paragraphs (1) and (2) of this subsection, the court shall order the governmental entity to file a sworn response, which may be filed in camera if the governmental entity includes in its response the reasons which make in camera review appropriate. If the court is unable to determine the motion or application on the basis of the parties' initial allegations and response, the court may conduct such additional proceedings as it deems appropriate. All such proceedings shall be completed and the motion or application decided as soon as practicable after the filing of the governmental entity's response.

(4) If the court finds that the applicant is not the subscriber or customer for whom the communications sought by the governmental entity are maintained, or that there is a reason to believe that the law enforcement inquiry is legitimate and that the communications sought are relevant to that inquiry, it shall deny the motion or application and order such process enforced. If the court finds that the applicant is the subscriber or customer for whom the communications sought by the governmental entity are maintained, and that there is not a reason to believe that the communications sought are relevant to a legitimate law enforcement inquiry, or that there has not been substantial compliance with the provisions of this chapter, it shall order the process quashed.

(5) A court order denying a motion or application under this section shall not be deemed a final order and no interlocutory appeal may be taken therefrom by the customer.

18 U.S.C. § 2705. DELAYED NOTICE

(a) Delay of notification.

(1) A governmental entity acting under section 2703(b) of this title may—

(A) where a court order is sought, include in the application a request, which the court shall grant, for an order delaying the notification required under section 2703(b) of this title for a period not to exceed ninety days, if the court determines that there is reason to believe that notification of the existence of the court order may have an adverse result described in paragraph (2) of this subsection; or

(B) where an administrative subpoena authorized by a Federal or State statute or a Federal or State grand jury subpoena is obtained, delay the notification required under section 2703(b) of this title for a period not to exceed ninety days upon the execution of a written certification of a supervisory official that there is reason to believe that notification of the existence of the subpoena may have an adverse result described in paragraph (2) of this subsection.

(2) An adverse result for the purposes of paragraph (1) of this subsection is—

(A) endangering the life or physical safety of an individual;

(B) flight from prosecution;

(C) destruction of or tampering with evidence;

(D) intimidation of potential witnesses; or

(E) otherwise seriously jeopardizing an investigation or unduly delaying a trial.

(3) The governmental entity shall maintain a true copy of certification under paragraph (1)(B).

(4) Extensions of the delay of notification provided in section 2703 of up to ninety days each may be granted by the court upon application, or by certification by a governmental entity, but only in accordance with subsection (b) of this section.

(5) Upon expiration of the period of delay of notification under paragraph (1) or (4) of this subsection, the governmental entity shall serve upon, or deliver by registered or first-class mail to, the customer or subscriber a copy of the process or request together with notice that—

(A) states with reasonable specificity the nature of the law enforcement inquiry; and

(B) informs such customer or subscriber—

(i) that information maintained for such customer or subscriber by the service provider named in such process or request was supplied to or requested by that governmental authority and the date on which the supplying or request took place;

(ii) that notification of such customer or subscriber was delayed;

(iii) what governmental entity or court made the certification or determination pursuant to which that delay was made; and

(iv) which provision of this chapter allowed such delay.

(6) As used in this subsection, the term "supervisory official" means the investigative agent in charge or assistant investigative agent in charge or an equivalent of an investigating agency's headquarters or regional office, or the chief prosecuting attorney or the first assistant prosecuting attorney or an equivalent of a prosecuting attorney's headquarters or regional office.

(b) Preclusion of notice to subject of governmental access. A governmental entity acting under section 2703, when it is not required to notify the subscriber or customer under section 2703(b)(1), or to the extent that it may delay such notice pursuant to subsection (a) of this section, may apply to a court for an order commanding a provider of electronic communications service or remote computing service to whom a warrant, subpoena, or court order is directed, for such period as the court deems appropriate, not to notify any other person of the existence of the warrant, subpoena, or court order. The court shall enter such an order if it determines that there is reason to believe that notification of the existence of the warrant, subpoena, or court order will result in—

(1) endangering the life or physical safety of an individual;

(2) flight from prosecution;

(3) destruction of or tampering with evidence;

(4) intimidation of potential witnesses; or

(5) otherwise seriously jeopardizing an investigation or unduly delaying a trial.

18 U.S.C. § 2706. COST REIMBURSEMENT

(a) Payment. Except as otherwise provided in subsection (c), a governmental entity obtaining the contents of communications, records, or other information under section 2702, 2703, or 2704 of this title shall pay to the person or entity assembling or providing such information a fee for reimbursement for such costs as are reasonably necessary and which have been directly incurred in searching for, assembling, reproducing, or otherwise providing such information. Such reimbursable costs shall include any costs due to necessary disruption of normal operations of any electronic communication service or remote computing service in which such information may be stored.

(b) Amount. The amount of the fee provided by subsection (a) shall be as mutually agreed by the governmental entity and the person or entity providing the information, or, in the absence of agreement, shall be as determined by the court which issued the order for production of such information (or the court before which a criminal prosecution relating to such information would be brought, if no court order was issued for production of the information).

(c) Exception. The requirement of subsection (a) of this section does not apply with respect to records or other information maintained by a communications common carrier that relate to telephone toll records and telephone listings obtained under section 2703 of this title. The court may, however, order a payment as described in subsection (a) if the court determines the information required is unusually voluminous in nature or otherwise caused an undue burden on the provider.

18 U.S.C. § 2707. CIVIL ACTION

(a) Cause of action. Except as provided in section 2703(e), any provider of electronic communication service, subscriber, or other person aggrieved by any violation of this chapter in which the conduct constituting the violation is engaged in with a knowing or intentional state of mind may, in a civil action, recover from the person or entity, other than the United States, which engaged in that violation such relief as may be appropriate.

(b) Relief. In a civil action under this section, appropriate relief includes—

    (1) such preliminary and other equitable or declaratory relief as may be appropriate;

    (2) damages under subsection (c); and

    (3) a reasonable attorney's fee and other litigation costs reasonably incurred.

(c) Damages. The court may assess as damages in a civil action under this section the sum of the actual damages suffered by the plaintiff and any profits made by the violator as a result of the violation, but in no case shall a person entitled to recover receive less than the sum of $1,000. If the violation is willful or intentional, the court may assess punitive damages. In the case of a successful action to enforce liability under this section, the court may assess the costs of the action, together with reasonable attorney fees determined by the court.

(d) Administrative discipline. If a court or appropriate department or agency determines that the United States or any of its departments or agencies has violated any provision of this chapter, and the court or appropriate department or agency finds that the circumstances surrounding the violation raise serious questions about whether or not an officer or employee of the United States acted willfully or intentionally with respect to the violation, the department or agency shall, upon receipt of a true and correct copy of the decision and findings of the court or appropriate department or agency promptly initiate a proceeding to determine whether disciplinary action against the officer or employee is warranted. If the head of the department or agency involved determines that disciplinary action is not warranted, he or she shall notify the Inspector General with jurisdiction over the department or agency concerned and shall provide the Inspector General with the reasons for such determination.

(e) Defense. A good faith reliance on—

    (1) a court warrant or order, a grand jury subpoena, a legislative authorization, or a statutory authorization (including a request of a governmental entity under section 2703(f) of this title);

(2) a request of an investigative or law enforcement officer under section 2518(7) of this title; or

(3) a good faith determination that section 2511(3), section 2702(b)(9), or section 2702(c)(7) of this title permitted the conduct complained of;

is a complete defense to any civil or criminal action brought under this chapter or any other law.

(f) Limitation. A civil action under this section may not be commenced later than two years after the date upon which the claimant first discovered or had a reasonable opportunity to discover the violation.

(g) Improper disclosure. Any willful disclosure of a 'record', as that term is defined in section 552a(a) of title 5, United States Code, obtained by an investigative or law enforcement officer, or a governmental entity, pursuant to section 2703 of this title, or from a device installed pursuant to section 3123 or 3125 of this title, that is not a disclosure made in the proper performance of the official functions of the officer or governmental entity making the disclosure, is a violation of this chapter. This provision shall not apply to information previously lawfully disclosed (prior to the commencement of any civil or administrative proceeding under this chapter) to the public by a Federal, State, or local governmental entity or by the plaintiff in a civil action under this chapter.

18 U.S.C. § 2708. EXCLUSIVITY OF REMEDIES

The remedies and sanctions described in this chapter are the only judicial remedies and sanctions for nonconstitutional violations of this chapter.

18 U.S.C. § 2711. DEFINITIONS FOR CHAPTER

As used in this chapter—

(1) the terms defined in section 2510 of this title have, respectively, the definitions given such terms in that section;

(2) the term "remote computing service" means the provision to the public of computer storage or processing services by means of an electronic communications system;

(3) the term "court of competent jurisdiction" includes—

(A) any district court of the United States (including a magistrate judge of such a court) or any United States court of appeals that—(i) has jurisdiction over the offense being investigated; (ii) is in or for a district in which the provider of a wire or electronic communication service is located or in which the wire or electronic communications, records, or other information are stored; or (iii) is acting on a request for foreign assistance pursuant to section 3512 of this title; or

(B) a court of general criminal jurisdiction of a State authorized by the law of that State to issue search warrants; and

(4) the term "governmental entity" means a department or agency of the United States or any State or political subdivision thereof.

18 U.S.C. § 2713. REQUIRED PRESERVATION AND DISCLOSURE OF COMMUNICATIONS AND RECORDS

A provider of electronic communication service or remote computing service shall comply with the obligations of this chapter to preserve, backup, or disclose the contents of a wire or electronic communication and any record or other information pertaining to a customer or subscriber within such provider's possession, custody, or control, regardless of whether such communication, record, or other information is located within or outside of the United States.

18 U.S.C. § 3121. GENERAL PROHIBITION ON PEN REGISTER AND TRAP AND TRACE DEVICE USE; EXCEPTION

(a) In general. Except as provided in this section, no person may install or use a pen register or a trap and trace device without first obtaining a court order under section 3123 of this title or under the Foreign Intelligence Surveillance Act of 1978 (50 U.S.C. 1801 et seq.) or an order from a foreign government that is subject to an executive agreement that the Attorney General has determined and certified to Congress satisfies section 2523.

(b) Exception. The prohibition of subsection (a) does not apply with respect to the use of a pen register or a trap and trace device by a provider of electronic or wire communication service—

(1) relating to the operation, maintenance, and testing of a wire or electronic communication service or to the protection of the rights or property of such provider, or to the protection of users of that service from abuse of service or unlawful use of service; or

(2) to record the fact that a wire or electronic communication was initiated or completed in order to protect such provider, another provider furnishing service toward the completion of the wire communication, or a user of that service, from fraudulent, unlawful or abusive use of service; or

(3) where the consent of the user of that service has been obtained.

(c) Limitation. A government agency authorized to install and use a pen register or trap and trace device under this chapter or under State law shall use technology reasonably available to it that restricts the recording or decoding of electronic or other impulses to the dialing, routing, addressing, and signaling information utilized in the processing and transmitting of wire or electronic communications so as not to include the contents of any wire or electronic communications.

(d) Penalty. Whoever knowingly violates subsection (a) shall be fined under this title or imprisoned not more than one year, or both.

18 U.S.C. § 3122. APPLICATION FOR AN ORDER FOR A PEN REGISTER OR A TRAP AND TRACE DEVICE

(a) Application.

(1) An attorney for the Government may make application for an order or an extension of an order under section 3123 of this title authorizing or approving the installation and use of a pen register or a trap and trace device under this chapter, in writing under oath or equivalent affirmation, to a court of competent jurisdiction.

(2) Unless prohibited by State law, a State investigative or law enforcement officer may make application for an order or an extension of an order under section 3123 of this title authorizing or approving the installation and use of a pen register or a trap and trace device under this chapter, in writing under oath or equivalent affirmation, to a court of competent jurisdiction of such State.

(b) Contents of application. An application under subsection (a) of this section shall include—

(1) the identity of the attorney for the Government or the State law enforcement or investigative officer making the application and the identity of the law enforcement agency conducting the investigation; and

(2) a certification by the applicant that the information likely to be obtained is relevant to an ongoing criminal investigation being conducted by that agency.

18 U.S.C. § 3123. ISSUANCE OF AN ORDER FOR A PEN REGISTER OR A TRAP AND TRACE DEVICE

(a) In general.

(1) Attorney for the Government. Upon an application made under section 3122(a)(1), the court shall enter an ex parte order authorizing the installation and use of a pen register or trap and trace device anywhere within the United States, if the court finds that the attorney for the Government has certified to the court that the information likely to be obtained by such installation and use is relevant to an ongoing criminal investigation. The order, upon service of that order, shall apply to any person or entity providing wire or electronic communication service in the United States whose assistance may facilitate the execution of the order. Whenever such an order is served on any person or entity not specifically named in the order, upon request of such person or entity, the attorney for the Government or law enforcement or investigative officer that is serving the order shall provide written or electronic certification that the order applies to the person or entity being served.

(2) **State investigative or law enforcement officer.** Upon an application made under section 3122(a)(2), the court shall enter an ex parte order authorizing the installation and use of a pen register or trap and trace device within the jurisdiction of the court, if the court finds that the State law enforcement or investigative officer has certified to the court that the information likely to be obtained by such installation and use is relevant to an ongoing criminal investigation.

(3)(A)   Where the law enforcement agency implementing an ex parte order under this subsection seeks to do so by installing and using its own pen register or trap and trace device on a packet-switched data network of a provider of electronic communication service to the public, the agency shall ensure that a record will be maintained which will identify—

> (i)   any officer or officers who installed the device and any officer or officers who accessed the device to obtain information from the network;

> (ii)   the date and time the device was installed, the date and time the device was uninstalled, and the date, time, and duration of each time the device is accessed to obtain information;

> (iii) the configuration of the device at the time of its installation and any subsequent modification thereof; and

> (iv) any information which has been collected by the device.

To the extent that the pen register or trap and trace device can be set automatically to record this information electronically, the record shall be maintained electronically throughout the installation and use of such device.

> (B) The record maintained under subparagraph (A) shall be provided ex parte and under seal to the court which entered the ex parte order authorizing the installation and use of the device within 30 days after termination of the order (including any extensions thereof).

(b) **Contents of order.** An order issued under this section—

(1) shall specify—

(A) the identity, if known, of the person to whom is leased or in whose name is listed the telephone line or other facility to which the pen register or trap and trace device is to be attached or applied;

(B) the identity, if known, of the person who is the subject of the criminal investigation;

(C) the attributes of the communications to which the order applies, including the number or other identifier and, if known, the location of the telephone line or other facility to which the pen register or trap and trace device is to be attached or applied, and, in the case of an order authorizing installation and use of a trap and trace device under subsection (a)(2), the geographic limits of the order; and

(D) a statement of the offense to which the information likely to be obtained by the pen register or trap and trace device relates; and

(2) shall direct, upon the request of the applicant, the furnishing of information, facilities, and technical assistance necessary to accomplish the installation of the pen register or trap and trace device under section 3124 of this title.

(c) Time period and extensions.

(1) An order issued under this section shall authorize the installation and use of a pen register or a trap and trace device for a period not to exceed sixty days.

(2) Extensions of such an order may be granted, but only upon an application for an order under section 3122 of this title and upon the judicial finding required by subsection (a) of this section. The period of extension shall be for a period not to exceed sixty days.

(d) Nondisclosure of existence of pen register or a trap and trace device. An order authorizing or approving the installation and use of a pen register or a trap and trace device shall direct that

(1) the order be sealed until otherwise ordered by the court; and

(2) the person owning or leasing the line or other facility to which the pen register or a trap and trace device is attached, or applied, or who is obligated by the order to provide assistance to the applicant, not disclose the existence of the pen register or trap and trace device or the existence of the investigation to the listed subscriber, or to any other person, unless or until otherwise ordered by the court.

18 U.S.C. § 3124. ASSISTANCE IN INSTALLATION AND USE OF A PEN REGISTER OR A TRAP AND TRACE DEVICE

(a) Pen registers. Upon the request of an attorney for the Government or an officer of a law enforcement agency authorized to install and use a pen register under this chapter, a provider of wire or electronic communication service, landlord, custodian, or other person shall furnish such investigative or law enforcement officer forthwith all information, facilities, and technical assistance necessary to accomplish the installation of the pen register unobtrusively and with a minimum of interference with the services that the person so ordered by the court accords the party with respect to whom the installation and use is to take place, if such assistance is directed by a court order as provided in section 3123(b)(2) of this title.

(b) Trap and trace device. Upon the request of an attorney for the Government or an officer of a law enforcement agency authorized to receive the results of a trap and trace device under this chapter, a provider of a wire or electronic communication service, landlord, custodian, or other person shall install such device forthwith on the appropriate line or other facility and shall furnish such investigative or law enforcement officer all additional information, facilities and technical assistance including installation and operation of the device unobtrusively and with a minimum of interference with the services that the person so ordered by the court accords the party with respect to whom the installation and use is to take place, if such installation and assistance is directed by a court order as provided in section 3123(b)(2) of this title. Unless otherwise ordered by the court, the results of the trap and trace device shall be furnished, pursuant to section 3123(b) or section 3125 of this title, to the officer of a law enforcement agency, designated in the court order, at reasonable intervals during regular business hours for the duration of the order.

(c) Compensation. A provider of a wire or electronic communication service, landlord, custodian, or other person who furnishes facilities or technical assistance pursuant to this section shall be reasonably compensated for such reasonable expenses incurred in providing such facilities and assistance.

(d) No cause of action against a provider disclosing information under this chapter. No cause of action shall lie in any court against any provider of a wire or electronic communication service, its officers, employees, agents, or other specified persons for providing information, facilities, or assistance in accordance with a court order under this chapter, request pursuant to section 3125 of this title, or an order from a foreign government that is subject to an executive agreement that the Attorney General has determined and certified to Congress satisfies section 2523.

(e) **Defense.** A good faith reliance on a court order under this chapter, a request pursuant to section 3125 of this title, a legislative authorization, a statutory authorization, or a good faith determination that the conduct complained of was permitted by an order from a foreign government that is subject to executive agreement that the Attorney General has determined and certified to Congress satisfies section 2523, is a complete defense against any civil or criminal action brought under this chapter or any other law.

(f) **Communications assistance enforcement orders.** Pursuant to section 2522, an order may be issued to enforce the assistance capability and capacity requirements under the Communications Assistance for Law Enforcement Act.

18 U.S.C. § 3125. EMERGENCY PEN REGISTER AND TRAP AND TRACE DEVICE INSTALLATION

(a) Notwithstanding any other provision of this chapter, any investigative or law enforcement officer, specially designated by the Attorney General, the Deputy Attorney General, the Associate Attorney General, any Assistant Attorney General, any acting Assistant Attorney General, or any Deputy Assistant Attorney General, or by the principal prosecuting attorney of any State or subdivision thereof acting pursuant to a statute of that State, who reasonably determines that—

(1) an emergency situation exists that involves—

(A) immediate danger of death or serious bodily injury to any person;

(B) conspiratorial activities characteristic of organized crime;

(C) an immediate threat to a national security interest; or

(D) an ongoing attack on a protected computer (as defined in section 1030) that constitutes a crime punishable by a term of imprisonment greater than one year;

that requires the installation and use of a pen register or a trap and trace device before an order authorizing such installation and use can, with due diligence, be obtained, and

(2) there are grounds upon which an order could be entered under this chapter to authorize such installation and use;

may have installed and use a pen register or trap and trace device if, within forty-eight hours after the installation has occurred, or begins to occur, an order approving the installation or use is issued in accordance with section 3123 of this title.

(b) In the absence of an authorizing order, such use shall immediately terminate when the information sought is obtained, when the application for the order is denied or when forty-eight hours have lapsed since the installation of the pen register or trap and trace device, whichever is earlier.

(c) The knowing installation or use by any investigative or law enforcement officer of a pen register or trap and trace device pursuant to subsection (a) without application for the authorizing order within forty-eight hours of the installation shall constitute a violation of this chapter.

(d) A provider of a wire or electronic service, landlord, custodian, or other person who furnished facilities or technical assistance pursuant to this section shall be reasonably compensated for such reasonable expenses incurred in providing such facilities and assistance.

18 U.S.C. § 3126. REPORTS CONCERNING PEN REGISTERS AND TRAP AND TRACE DEVICES

The Attorney General shall annually report to Congress on the number of pen register orders and orders for trap and trace devices applied for by law enforcement agencies of the Department of Justice, which report shall include information concerning—

(1) the period of interceptions authorized by the order, and the number and duration of any extensions of the order;

(2) the offense specified in the order or application, or extension of an order;

(3) the number of investigations involved;

(4) the number and nature of the facilities affected; and

(5) the identity, including district, of the applying investigative or law enforcement agency making the application and the person authorizing the order.

18 U.S.C. § 3127. DEFINITIONS FOR CHAPTER

As used in this chapter—

(1) the terms "wire communication", "electronic communication", "electronic communication service", and "contents" have the meanings set forth for such terms in section 2510 of this title;

(2) the term "court of competent jurisdiction" means—

(A) any district court of the United States (including a magistrate judge of such a court) or any United States court of appeals that—(i) has jurisdiction over the offense being investigated; (ii) is in or for a district in which the provider of a wire or electronic communication service is located; (iii) is in or for a district in which a landlord, custodian, or other person subject to subsections (a) or (b) of section 3124 of this title is located; or (iv) is acting on a request for foreign assistance pursuant to section 3512 of this title; or

(B) a court of general criminal jurisdiction of a State authorized by the law of that State to enter orders authorizing the use of a pen register or a trap and trace device;

(3) the term "pen register" means a device or process which records or decodes dialing, routing, addressing, or signaling information transmitted by an instrument or facility from which a wire or electronic communication is transmitted, provided, however, that such information shall not include the contents of any communication, but such term does not include any device or process used by a provider or customer of a wire or electronic communication service for billing, or recording as an incident to billing, for communications services provided by such provider or any device or process used by a provider or customer of a wire communication service for cost accounting or other like purposes in the ordinary course of its business;

(4) the term "trap and trace device" means a device or process which captures the incoming electronic or other impulses which identify the originating number or other dialing, routing, addressing, and signaling information reasonably likely to identify the source of a wire or electronic communication, provided, however, that such information shall not include the contents of any communication;

(5) the term "attorney for the Government" has the meaning given such term for the purposes of the Federal Rules of Criminal Procedure; and

(6) the term "State" means a State, the District of Columbia, Puerto Rico, and any other possession or territory of the United States.

47 U.S.C. § 223. OBSCENE OR HARASSING TELEPHONE CALLS IN THE DISTRICT OF COLUMBIA OR IN INTERSTATE OR FOREIGN COMMUNICATIONS

(a) Prohibited acts generally. Whoever—

(1) in interstate or foreign communications—

(A) by means of a telecommunications device knowingly—

(i) makes, creates, or solicits, and

(ii) initiates the transmission of,

any comment, request, suggestion, proposal, image, or other communication which is obscene or child pornography, with intent to annoy, abuse, threaten, or harass another person;

(B) by means of a telecommunications device knowingly—

(i) makes, creates, or solicits, and

(ii) initiates the transmission of,

any comment, request, suggestion, proposal, image, or other communication which is obscene or child pornography, knowing that the recipient of the communication is under 18 years of age, regardless of whether the maker of such communication placed the call or initiated the communication;

(C) makes a telephone call or utilizes a telecommunications device, whether or not conversation or communication ensues, without disclosing his identity and with intent to annoy, abuse, threaten, or harass any person at the called number or who receives the communications;

(D) makes or causes the telephone of another repeatedly or continuously to ring, with intent to harass any person at the called number; or

(E) makes repeated telephone calls or repeatedly initiates communication with a telecommunications device, during which conversation or communication ensues, solely to harass any person at the called number or who receives the communication; or

(2) knowingly permits any telecommunications facility under his control to be used for any activity prohibited by paragraph (1) with the intent that it be used for such activity,

shall be fined under Title 18 or imprisoned not more than two years, or both.

(b) Prohibited acts for commercial purposes; defense to prosecution.

(1) Whoever knowingly—

(A) within the United States, by means of telephone, makes (directly or by recording device) any obscene communication for commercial purposes to any person, regardless of whether the maker of such communication placed the call; or

(B) permits any telephone facility under such person's control to be used for an activity prohibited by subparagraph (A),

shall be fined in accordance with Title 18 or imprisoned not more than two years, or both.

(2) Whoever knowingly—

(A) within the United States, by means of telephone, makes (directly or by recording device) any indecent communication for commercial purposes which is available to any person under 18 years of age or to any other person without that person's consent, regardless of whether the maker of such communication placed the call; or

(B) permits any telephone facility under such person's control to be used for an activity prohibited by subparagraph (A), shall be fined not more than $50,000 or imprisoned not more than six months, or both.

(3) It is a defense to prosecution under paragraph (2) of this subsection that the defendant restricted access to the prohibited communication to persons 18 years of age or older in accordance with subsection (c) of this section and with such procedures as the Commission may prescribe by regulation.

(4) In addition to the penalties under paragraph (1), whoever, within the United States, intentionally violates paragraph (1) or (2) shall be subject to a fine of not more than $50,000 for each violation. For purposes of this paragraph, each day of violation shall constitute a separate violation.

(5)(A) In addition to the penalties under paragraphs (1), (2), and (5), whoever, within the United States, violates paragraph (1) or (2) shall be subject to a civil fine of not more than $50,000 for each violation. For purposes of this paragraph, each day of violation shall constitute a separate violation.

(B) A fine under this paragraph may be assessed either—

(i) by a court, pursuant to civil action by the Commission or any attorney employed by the Commission who is designated by the Commission for such purposes, or

(ii) by the Commission after appropriate administrative proceedings.

(6) The Attorney General may bring a suit in the appropriate district court of the United States to enjoin any act or practice which violates paragraph (1) or (2). An injunction may be granted in accordance with the Federal Rules of Civil Procedure.

(c) Restriction on access to subscribers by common carriers; judicial remedies respecting restrictions.

(1) A common carrier within the District of Columbia or within any State, or in interstate or foreign commerce, shall not, to the extent technically feasible, provide access to a communication specified in subsection (b) of this section from the telephone of any subscriber who has not previously requested in writing the carrier to provide access to such communication if the carrier collects from subscribers an identifiable charge for such communication that the carrier remits, in whole or in part, to the provider of such communication.

(2) Except as provided in paragraph (3), no cause of action may be brought in any court or administrative agency against any common carrier, or any of its affiliates, including their officers, directors, employees, agents, or authorized representatives on account of—

> **(A)** any action which the carrier demonstrates was taken in good faith to restrict access pursuant to paragraph (1) of this subsection; or

> **(B)** any access permitted—

>> **(i)** in good faith reliance upon the lack of any representation by a provider of communications that communications provided by that provider are communications specified in subsection (b) of this section, or

>> **(ii)** because a specific representation by the provider did not allow the carrier, acting in good faith, a sufficient period to restrict access to communications described in subsection (b) of this section.

(3) Notwithstanding paragraph (2) of this subsection, a provider of communications services to which subscribers are denied access pursuant to paragraph (1) of this subsection may bring an action for a declaratory judgment or similar action in a court. Any such action shall be limited to the question of whether the communications which the provider seeks to provide fall within the category of communications to which the carrier will provide access only to subscribers who have previously requested such access.

(d) Sending or displaying offensive material to persons under 18. Whoever—

> **(1)** in interstate or foreign communications knowingly—

>> **(A)** uses an interactive computer service to send to a specific person or persons under 18 years of age, or

>> **(B)** uses any interactive computer service to display in a manner available to a person under 18 years of age,

any comment, request, suggestion, proposal, image, or other communication that, is obscene or child pornography, regardless of whether the user of such service placed the call or initiated the communication; or

(2) knowingly permits any telecommunications facility under such person's control to be used for an activity prohibited by paragraph (1) with the intent that it be used for such activity,

shall be fined under Title 18 or imprisoned not more than two years, or both.

(e) Defenses. In addition to any other defenses available by law:

(1) No person shall be held to have violated subsection (a) or (d) of this section solely for providing access or connection to or from a facility, system, or network not under that person's control, including transmission, downloading, intermediate storage, access software, or other related capabilities that are incidental to providing such access or connection that does not include the creation of the content of the communication.

(2) The defenses provided by paragraph (1) of this subsection shall not be applicable to a person who is a conspirator with an entity actively involved in the creation or knowing distribution of communications that violate this section, or who knowingly advertises the availability of such communications.

(3) The defenses provided in paragraph (1) of this subsection shall not be applicable to a person who provides access or connection to a facility, system, or network engaged in the violation of this section that is owned or controlled by such person.

(4) No employer shall be held liable under this section for the actions of an employee or agent unless the employee's or agent's conduct is within the scope of his or her employment or agency and the employer (A) having knowledge of such conduct, authorizes or ratifies such conduct, or (B) recklessly disregards such conduct.

(5) It is a defense to a prosecution under subsection (a)(1)(B) or (d) of this section, or under subsection (a)(2) of this section with respect to the use of a facility for an activity under subsection (a)(1)(B) of this section that a person—

(A) has taken, in good faith, reasonable, effective, and appropriate actions under the circumstances to restrict or prevent access by minors to a communication specified in such subsections, which may involve any appropriate measures to restrict minors from such communications, including any method which is feasible under available technology; or

(B) has restricted access to such communication by requiring use of a verified credit card, debit account, adult access code, or adult personal identification number.

(6) The Commission may describe measures which are reasonable, effective, and appropriate to restrict access to prohibited communications under subsection (d) of this section. Nothing in this section authorizes the Commission to enforce, or is intended to provide the Commission with the authority to approve, sanction, or permit, the use of such measures. The Commission shall have no enforcement authority over the failure to utilize such measures. The Commission shall not endorse specific products relating to such measures. The use of such measures shall be admitted as evidence of good faith efforts for purposes of paragraph (5) in any action arising under subsection (d) of this section. Nothing in this section shall be construed to treat interactive computer services as common carriers or telecommunications carriers.

(f) Violations of law required; commercial entities, nonprofit libraries, or institutions of higher education.

(1) No cause of action may be brought in any court or administrative agency against any person on account of any activity that is not in violation of any law punishable by criminal or civil penalty, and that the person has taken in good faith to implement a defense authorized under this section or otherwise to restrict or prevent the transmission of, or access to, a communication specified in this section.

(2) No State or local government may impose any liability for commercial activities or actions by commercial entities, nonprofit libraries, or institutions of higher education in connection with an activity or action described in subsection (a)(2) or (d) of this section that is inconsistent with the treatment of those activities or actions under this section: *Provided, however*, That nothing herein shall preclude any State or local government from enacting and enforcing complementary oversight, liability, and regulatory systems, procedures, and requirements, so long as such systems, procedures, and requirements govern only intrastate services and do not result in the imposition of inconsistent rights, duties or obligations on the provision of interstate services. Nothing in this subsection shall preclude any State or local government from governing conduct not covered by this section.

(g) Application and enforcement of other Federal law. Nothing in subsection (a), (d), (e), or (f) of this section or in the defenses to prosecution under subsection (a) or (d) of this section shall be construed to affect or limit the application or enforcement of any other Federal law.

(h) Definitions. For purposes of this section—

(1) The use of the term "telecommunications device" in this section—

(A) shall not impose new obligations on broadcasting station licensees and cable operators covered by obscenity and indecency provisions elsewhere in this chapter;

(B) does not include an interactive computer service; and

(C) in the case of subparagraph (C) of subsection (a)(1), includes any device or software that can be used to originate telecommunications or other types of communications that are transmitted, in whole or in part, by the Internet (as such term is defined in section 1104 of the Internet Tax Freedom Act (47 U.S.C. 151 note)).

(2) The term "interactive computer service" has the meaning provided in section 230(f)(2) of this title.

(3) The term "access software" means software (including client or server software) or enabling tools that do not create or provide the content of the communication but that allow a user to do any one or more of the following:

(A) filter, screen, allow, or disallow content;

(B) pick, choose, analyze, or digest content; or

(C) transmit, receive, display, forward, cache, search, subset, organize, reorganize, or translate content.

(4) The term "institution of higher education" has the meaning provided in section 1001 of Title 20.

(5) The term "library" means a library eligible for participation in State-based plans for funds under title III of the Library Services and Construction Act (20 U.S.C. 355e et seq.).

CYBERSECURITY ACT OF 2015

6 U.S.C. § 1501. DEFINITIONS

In this subchapter:

* * *

(4) Cybersecurity purpose

The term "cybersecurity purpose" means the purpose of protecting an information system or information that is stored on, processed by, or transiting an information system from a cybersecurity threat or security vulnerability.

(5) Cybersecurity threat

(A) In general

Except as provided in subparagraph (B), the term "cybersecurity threat" means an action, not protected by the First Amendment to the

Constitution of the United States, on or through an information system that may result in an unauthorized effort to adversely impact the security, availability, confidentiality, or integrity of an information system or information that is stored on, processed by, or transiting an information system.

(B) Exclusion

The term "cybersecurity threat" does not include any action that solely involves a violation of a consumer term of service or a consumer licensing agreement.

(6) Cyber threat indicator

The term "cyber threat indicator" means information that is necessary to describe or identify—

(A) malicious reconnaissance, including anomalous patterns of communications that appear to be transmitted for the purpose of gathering technical information related to a cybersecurity threat or security vulnerability;

(B) a method of defeating a security control or exploitation of a security vulnerability;

(C) a security vulnerability, including anomalous activity that appears to indicate the existence of a security vulnerability;

(D) a method of causing a user with legitimate access to an information system or information that is stored on, processed by, or transiting an information system to unwittingly enable the defeat of a security control or exploitation of a security vulnerability;

(E) malicious cyber command and control;

(F) the actual or potential harm caused by an incident, including a description of the information exfiltrated as a result of a particular cybersecurity threat;

(G) any other attribute of a cybersecurity threat, if disclosure of such attribute is not otherwise prohibited by law; or

(H) any combination thereof.

(7) Defensive measure

(A) In general

Except as provided in subparagraph (B), the term "defensive measure" means an action, device, procedure, signature, technique, or other measure applied to an information system or information that is stored on, processed by, or transiting an information system that detects, prevents, or mitigates a known or suspected cybersecurity threat or security vulnerability.

(B) Exclusion

The term "defensive measure" does not include a measure that destroys, renders unusable, provides unauthorized access to, or substantially harms an information system or information stored on, processed by, or transiting such information system not owned by—

(i) the private entity operating the measure; or

(ii) another entity or Federal entity that is authorized to provide consent and has provided consent to that private entity for operation of such measure.

(8) Federal entity

The term "Federal entity" means a department or agency of the United States or any component of such department or agency.

(9) Information system

The term "information system"—

(A) has the meaning given the term in section 3502 of Title 44; and

(B) includes industrial control systems, such as supervisory control and data acquisition systems, distributed control systems, and programmable logic controllers.

(10) Local government

The term "local government" means any borough, city, county, parish, town, township, village, or other political subdivision of a State.

(11) Malicious cyber command and control

The term "malicious cyber command and control" means a method for unauthorized remote identification of, access to, or use of, an information system or information that is stored on, processed by, or transiting an information system.

(12) Malicious reconnaissance

The term "malicious reconnaissance" means a method for actively probing or passively monitoring an information system for the purpose of discerning security vulnerabilities of the information system, if such method is associated with a known or suspected cybersecurity threat.

(13) Monitor

The term "monitor" means to acquire, identify, or scan, or to possess, information that is stored on, processed by, or transiting an information system.

(14) Non-Federal entity

(A) In general

Except as otherwise provided in this paragraph, the term "non-Federal entity" means any private entity, non-Federal government agency or department, or State, tribal, or local government (including a political subdivision, department, or component thereof).

(B) Inclusions

The term "non-Federal entity" includes a government agency or department of the District of Columbia, the Commonwealth of Puerto Rico, the United States Virgin Islands, Guam, American Samoa, the Northern Mariana Islands, and any other territory or possession of the United States.

(C) Exclusion

The term "non-Federal entity" does not include a foreign power as defined in section 1801 of Title 50.

(15) Private entity

(A) In general

Except as otherwise provided in this paragraph, the term "private entity" means any person or private group, organization, proprietorship, partnership, trust, cooperative, corporation, or other commercial or nonprofit entity, including an officer, employee, or agent thereof.

(B) Inclusion

The term "private entity" includes a State, tribal, or local government performing utility services, such as electric, natural gas, or water services.

(C) Exclusion

The term "private entity" does not include a foreign power as defined in section 1801 of Title 50.

(16) Security control

The term "security control" means the management, operational, and technical controls used to protect against an unauthorized effort to adversely affect the confidentiality, integrity, and availability of an information system or its information.

(17) Security vulnerability

The term "security vulnerability" means any attribute of hardware, software, process, or procedure that could enable or facilitate the defeat of a security control.

6 U.S.C. § 1503. AUTHORIZATIONS FOR PREVENTING, DETECTING, ANALYZING, AND MITIGATING CYBERSECURITY THREATS

(a) Authorization for monitoring

(1) In general

Notwithstanding any other provision of law, a private entity may, for cybersecurity purposes, monitor—

(A) an information system of such private entity;

(B) an information system of another non-Federal entity, upon the authorization and written consent of such other entity;

(C) an information system of a Federal entity, upon the authorization and written consent of an authorized representative of the Federal entity; and

(D) information that is stored on, processed by, or transiting an information system monitored by the private entity under this paragraph.

(2) Construction

Nothing in this subsection shall be construed—

(A) to authorize the monitoring of an information system, or the use of any information obtained through such monitoring, other than as provided in this subchapter; or

(B) to limit otherwise lawful activity.

(b) Authorization for operation of defensive measures

(1) In general

Notwithstanding any other provision of law, a private entity may, for cybersecurity purposes, operate a defensive measure that is applied to—

(A) an information system of such private entity in order to protect the rights or property of the private entity;

(B) an information system of another non-Federal entity upon written consent of such entity for operation of such defensive measure to protect the rights or property of such entity; and

(C) an information system of a Federal entity upon written consent of an authorized representative of such Federal entity for operation of such defensive measure to protect the rights or property of the Federal Government.

(2) Construction

Nothing in this subsection shall be construed—

(A) to authorize the use of a defensive measure other than as provided in this subsection; or

(B) to limit otherwise lawful activity.

(c) Authorization for sharing or receiving cyber threat indicators or defensive measures

(1) In general

Except as provided in paragraph (2) and notwithstanding any other provision of law, a non-Federal entity may, for a cybersecurity purpose and consistent with the protection of classified information, share with, or receive from, any other non-Federal entity or the Federal Government a cyber threat indicator or defensive measure.

(2) Lawful restriction

A non-Federal entity receiving a cyber threat indicator or defensive measure from another non-Federal entity or a Federal entity shall comply with otherwise lawful restrictions placed on the sharing or use of such cyber threat indicator or defensive measure by the sharing non-Federal entity or Federal entity.

(3) Construction

Nothing in this subsection shall be construed—

(A) to authorize the sharing or receiving of a cyber threat indicator or defensive measure other than as provided in this subsection; or

(B) to limit otherwise lawful activity.

(d) Protection and use of information

(1) Security of information

A non-Federal entity monitoring an information system, operating a defensive measure, or providing or receiving a cyber threat indicator or defensive measure under this section shall implement and utilize a security control to protect against unauthorized access to or acquisition of such cyber threat indicator or defensive measure.

(2) Removal of certain personal information

A non-Federal entity sharing a cyber threat indicator pursuant to this subchapter shall, prior to such sharing—

(A) review such cyber threat indicator to assess whether such cyber threat indicator contains any information not directly related to a cybersecurity threat that the non-Federal entity knows at the time of sharing to be personal information of a specific individual or information that identifies a specific individual and remove such information; or

(B) implement and utilize a technical capability configured to remove any information not directly related to a cybersecurity threat that the non-Federal entity knows at the time of sharing to be personal information of a specific individual or information that identifies a specific individual.

(3) Use of cyber threat indicators and defensive measures by non-Federal entities

(A) In general

Consistent with this subchapter, a cyber threat indicator or defensive measure shared or received under this section may, for cybersecurity purposes—

(i) be used by a non-Federal entity to monitor or operate a defensive measure that is applied to—

(I) an information system of the non-Federal entity; or

(II) an information system of another non-Federal entity or a Federal entity upon the written consent of that other non-Federal entity or that Federal entity; and

(ii) be otherwise used, retained, and further shared by a non-Federal entity subject to—

(I) an otherwise lawful restriction placed by the sharing non-Federal entity or Federal entity on such cyber threat indicator or defensive measure; or

(II) an otherwise applicable provision of law.

(B) Construction

Nothing in this paragraph shall be construed to authorize the use of a cyber threat indicator or defensive measure other than as provided in this section.

(4) Use of cyber threat indicators by State, tribal, or local government

(A) Law enforcement use

A State, tribal, or local government that receives a cyber threat indicator or defensive measure under this subchapter may use such cyber threat indicator or defensive measure for the purposes described in section 1504(d)(5)(A) of this title.

(B) Exemption from disclosure

A cyber threat indicator or defensive measure shared by or with a State, tribal, or local government, including a component of a State, tribal, or local government that is a private entity, under this section shall be—

(i) deemed voluntarily shared information; and

(ii) exempt from disclosure under any provision of State, tribal, or local freedom of information law, open government law, open meetings law, open records law, sunshine law, or similar law requiring disclosure of information or records.

(C) State, tribal, and local regulatory authority

(i) In general

Except as provided in clause (ii), a cyber threat indicator or defensive measure shared with a State, tribal, or local government under this subchapter shall not be used by any State, tribal, or local government to regulate, including an enforcement action, the lawful activity of any non-Federal entity or any activity taken by a non-Federal entity pursuant to mandatory standards, including an activity relating to monitoring, operating a defensive measure, or sharing of a cyber threat indicator.

(ii) Regulatory authority specifically relating to prevention or mitigation of cybersecurity threats

A cyber threat indicator or defensive measure shared as described in clause (i) may, consistent with a State, tribal, or local government regulatory authority specifically relating to the prevention or mitigation of cybersecurity threats to information systems, inform the development or implementation of a regulation relating to such information systems.

(e) Antitrust exemption

(1) In general

Except as provided in section 1507(e) of this title, it shall not be considered a violation of any provision of antitrust laws for 2 or more private entities to exchange or provide a cyber threat indicator or defensive measure, or assistance relating to the prevention, investigation, or mitigation of a cybersecurity threat, for cybersecurity purposes under this subchapter.

(2) Applicability

Paragraph (1) shall apply only to information that is exchanged or assistance provided in order to assist with—

(A) facilitating the prevention, investigation, or mitigation of a cybersecurity threat to an information system or information that is stored on, processed by, or transiting an information system; or

    (B) communicating or disclosing a cyber threat indicator to help prevent, investigate, or mitigate the effect of a cybersecurity threat to an information system or information that is stored on, processed by, or transiting an information system.

(f) No right or benefit

The sharing of a cyber threat indicator or defensive measure with a non-Federal entity under this subchapter shall not create a right or benefit to similar information by such non-Federal entity or any other non-Federal entity.

6 U.S.C. § 1505. PROTECTION FROM LIABILITY

(a) Monitoring of information systems

No cause of action shall lie or be maintained in any court against any private entity, and such action shall be promptly dismissed, for the monitoring of an information system and information under section 1503(a) of this title that is conducted in accordance with this subchapter.

(b) Sharing or receipt of cyber threat indicators

No cause of action shall lie or be maintained in any court against any private entity, and such action shall be promptly dismissed, for the sharing or receipt of a cyber threat indicator or defensive measure under section 1503(c) of this title if—

    (1) such sharing or receipt is conducted in accordance with this subchapter; and

    (2) in a case in which a cyber threat indicator or defensive measure is shared with the Federal Government, the cyber threat indicator or defensive measure is shared in a manner that is consistent with section 1504(c)(1)(B) of this title and the sharing or receipt, as the case may be, occurs after the earlier of—

        (A) the date on which the interim policies and procedures are submitted to Congress under section 1504(a)(1) of this title and guidelines are submitted to Congress under section 1504(b)(1) of this title; or

        (B) the date that is 60 days after December 18, 2015.

(c) Construction

Nothing in this subchapter shall be construed—

    (1) to create—

        (A) a duty to share a cyber threat indicator or defensive measure; or

(B) a duty to warn or act based on the receipt of a cyber threat indicator or defensive measure; or

(2) to undermine or limit the availability of otherwise applicable common law or statutory defenses.

6 U.S.C. § 1507. CONSTRUCTION AND PREEMPTION

(a) Otherwise lawful disclosures

Nothing in this subchapter shall be construed—

(1) to limit or prohibit otherwise lawful disclosures of communications, records, or other information, including reporting of known or suspected criminal activity, by a non-Federal entity to any other non-Federal entity or the Federal Government under this subchapter; or

(2) to limit or prohibit otherwise lawful use of such disclosures by any Federal entity, even when such otherwise lawful disclosures duplicate or replicate disclosures made under this subchapter.

(b) Whistle blower protections

Nothing in this subchapter shall be construed to prohibit or limit the disclosure of information protected under section 2302(b)(8) of Title 5 (governing disclosures of illegality, waste, fraud, abuse, or public health or safety threats), section 7211 of Title 5 (governing disclosures to Congress), section 1034 of Title 10 (governing disclosure to Congress by members of the military), section 3234 of Title 50 (governing disclosure by employees of elements of the intelligence community), or any similar provision of Federal or State law.

(c) Protection of sources and methods

Nothing in this subchapter shall be construed—

(1) as creating any immunity against, or otherwise affecting, any action brought by the Federal Government, or any agency or department thereof, to enforce any law, executive order, or procedure governing the appropriate handling, disclosure, or use of classified information;

(2) to affect the conduct of authorized law enforcement or intelligence activities; or

(3) to modify the authority of a department or agency of the Federal Government to protect classified information and sources and methods and the national security of the United States.

(d) Relationship to other laws

Nothing in this subchapter shall be construed to affect any requirement under any other provision of law for a non-Federal entity to provide information to the Federal Government.

(e) Prohibited conduct

Nothing in this subchapter shall be construed to permit price-fixing, allocating a market between competitors, monopolizing or attempting to monopolize a market, boycotting, or exchanges of price or cost information, customer lists, or information regarding future competitive planning.

(f) Information sharing relationships

Nothing in this subchapter shall be construed—

(1) to limit or modify an existing information sharing relationship;

(2) to prohibit a new information sharing relationship;

(3) to require a new information sharing relationship between any non-Federal entity and a Federal entity or another non-Federal entity; or

(4) to require the use of the capability and process within the Department of Homeland Security developed under section 1504(c) of this title.

(g) Preservation of contractual obligations and rights

Nothing in this subchapter shall be construed—

(1) to amend, repeal, or supersede any current or future contractual agreement, terms of service agreement, or other contractual relationship between any non-Federal entities, or between any non-Federal entity and a Federal entity; or

(2) to abrogate trade secret or intellectual property rights of any non-Federal entity or Federal entity.

(h) Anti-tasking restriction

Nothing in this subchapter shall be construed to permit a Federal entity—

(1) to require a non-Federal entity to provide information to a Federal entity or another non-Federal entity;

(2) to condition the sharing of cyber threat indicators with a non-Federal entity on such entity's provision of cyber threat indicators to a Federal entity or another non-Federal entity; or

(3) to condition the award of any Federal grant, contract, or purchase on the provision of a cyber threat indicator to a Federal entity or another non-Federal entity.

(i) No liability for non-participation

Nothing in this subchapter shall be construed to subject any entity to liability for choosing not to engage in the voluntary activities authorized in this subchapter.

(j) Use and retention of information

Nothing in this subchapter shall be construed to authorize, or to modify any existing authority of, a department or agency of the Federal Government to retain or use any information shared under this subchapter for any use other than permitted in this subchapter.

(k) Federal preemption

(1) In general

This subchapter supersedes any statute or other provision of law of a State or political subdivision of a State that restricts or otherwise expressly regulates an activity authorized under this subchapter.

(2) State law enforcement

Nothing in this subchapter shall be construed to supersede any statute or other provision of law of a State or political subdivision of a State concerning the use of authorized law enforcement practices and procedures.

(*l*) Regulatory authority

Nothing in this subchapter shall be construed—

(1) to authorize the promulgation of any regulations not specifically authorized to be issued under this subchapter;

(2) to establish or limit any regulatory authority not specifically established or limited under this subchapter; or

(3) to authorize regulatory actions that would duplicate or conflict with regulatory requirements, mandatory standards, or related processes under another provision of Federal law.

(m) Authority of Secretary of Defense to respond to malicious cyber activity carried out by foreign powers

Nothing in this subchapter shall be construed to limit the authority of the Secretary of Defense under section 394.

(n) Criminal prosecution

Nothing in this subchapter shall be construed to prevent the disclosure of a cyber threat indicator or defensive measure shared under this subchapter in a case of criminal prosecution, when an applicable provision of Federal, State, tribal, or local law requires disclosure in such case.

6 U.S.C. § 1510. EFFECTIVE PERIOD

(a) In general

Except as provided in subsection (b), this title and the amendments made by this title shall be effective during the period beginning on December 18, 2015, and ending on September 30, 2025.

(b) Exception

With respect to any action authorized by this subchapter or information obtained pursuant to an action authorized by this subchapter, which occurred before the date on which the provisions referred to in subsection (a) cease to have effect, the provisions of this subchapter shall continue in effect.

FEDERAL RULE OF CRIMINAL PROCEDURE 41
[Rule 41]

SEARCH AND SEIZURE

(Effective December 1, 2016)

(a) Scope and Definitions.

(1) Scope. This rule does not modify any statute regulating search or seizure, or the issuance and execution of a search warrant in special circumstances.

(2) Definitions. The following definitions apply under this rule:

(A) "Property" includes documents, books, papers, any other tangible objects, and information.

(B) "Daytime" means the hours between 6:00 a.m. and 10:00 p.m. according to local time.

(C) "Federal law enforcement officer" means a government agent (other than an attorney for the government) who is engaged in enforcing the criminal laws and is within any category of officers authorized by the Attorney General to request a search warrant.

(D) "Domestic terrorism" and "international terrorism" have the meanings set out in 18 U.S.C. § 2331.

(E) "Tracking device" has the meaning set out in 18 U.S.C. § 3117(b).

(b) Venue for a Warrant Application. At the request of a federal law enforcement officer or an attorney for the government:

(1) a magistrate judge with authority in the district—or if none is reasonably available, a judge of a state court of record in the district—has authority to issue a warrant to search for and seize a person or property located within the district;

(2) a magistrate judge with authority in the district has authority to issue a warrant for a person or property outside the district if the person or property is located within the district when the warrant is issued but might move or be moved outside the district before the warrant is executed;

(3) a magistrate judge—in an investigation of domestic terrorism or international terrorism—with authority in any district in which activities related to the terrorism may have occurred has authority to issue a warrant for a person or property within or outside that district;

(4) a magistrate judge with authority in the district has authority to issue a warrant to install within the district a tracking device; the warrant may authorize use of the device to track the movement of a person or property located within the district, outside the district, or both; and

(5) a magistrate judge having authority in any district where activities related to the crime may have occurred, or in the District of Columbia, may issue a warrant for property that is located outside the jurisdiction of any state or district, but within any of the following:

(A) a United States territory, possession, or commonwealth;

(B) the premises—no matter who owns them—of a United States diplomatic or consular mission in a foreign state, including any appurtenant building, part of a building, or land used for the mission's purposes; or

(C) a residence and any appurtenant land owned or leased by the United States and used by United States personnel assigned to a United States diplomatic or consular mission in a foreign state.

(6) a magistrate judge with authority in any district where activities related to a crime may have occurred has authority to issue a warrant to use remote access to search electronic storage media and to seize or copy electronically stored information located within or outside that district if:

(A) the district where the media or information is located has been concealed through technological means; or

(B) in an investigation of a violation of 18 U.S.C. § 1030(a)(5), the media are protected computers that have been damaged without authorization and are located in five or more districts.

(c) Persons or Property Subject to Search or Seizure. A warrant may be issued for any of the following:

(1) evidence of a crime;

(2) contraband, fruits of crime, or other items illegally possessed;

(3) property designed for use, intended for use, or used in committing a crime; or

(4) a person to be arrested or a person who is unlawfully restrained.

(d) Obtaining a Warrant.

(1) In General. After receiving an affidavit or other information, a magistrate judge—or if authorized by Rule 41(b), a judge of a state court of record—must issue the warrant if there is probable cause to search for and seize a person or property or to install and use a tracking device.

(2) Requesting a Warrant in the Presence of a Judge.

(A) *Warrant on an Affidavit.* When a federal law enforcement officer or an attorney for the government presents an affidavit in support of a warrant, the judge may require the affiant to appear personally and may examine under oath the affiant and any witness the affiant produces.

(B) *Warrant on Sworn Testimony.* The judge may wholly or partially dispense with a written affidavit and base a warrant on sworn testimony if doing so is reasonable under the circumstances.

(C) *Recording Testimony.* Testimony taken in support of a warrant must be recorded by a court reporter or by a suitable recording device, and the judge must file the transcript or recording with the clerk, along with any affidavit.

(3) Requesting a Warrant by Telephonic or Other Means.

(A) *In General.* A magistrate judge may issue a warrant based on information communicated by telephone or other reliable electronic means.

(B) *Recording Testimony.* Upon learning that an applicant is requesting a warrant under Rule 41(d)(3)(A), a magistrate judge must:

(i) place under oath the applicant and any person on whose testimony the application is based; and

(ii) make a verbatim record of the conversation with a suitable recording device, if available, or by a court reporter, or in writing.

(C) *Certifying Testimony.* The magistrate judge must have any recording or court reporter's notes transcribed, certify the transcription's accuracy, and file a copy of the record and the transcription with the clerk. Any written verbatim record must be signed by the magistrate judge and filed with the clerk.

(D) *Suppression Limited.* Absent a finding of bad faith, evidence obtained from a warrant issued under Rule 41(d)(3)(A) is not subject to suppression on the ground that issuing the warrant in that manner was unreasonable under the circumstances.

(e) Issuing the Warrant.

(1) In General. The magistrate judge or a judge of a state court of record must issue the warrant to an officer authorized to execute it.

(2) Contents of the Warrant.

(A) *Warrant to Search for and Seize a Person or Property.* Except for a tracking-device warrant, the warrant must identify the person or property to be searched, identify any person or property to be seized, and designate the magistrate judge to whom it must be returned. The warrant must command the officer to:

(i) execute the warrant within a specified time no longer than 14 days;

(ii) execute the warrant during the daytime, unless the judge for good cause expressly authorizes execution at another time; and

(iii) return the warrant to the magistrate judge designated in the warrant.

(B) *Warrant Seeking Electronically Stored Information.* A warrant under Rule 41(e)(2)(A) may authorize the seizure of electronic storage media or the seizure or copying of electronically stored information. Unless otherwise specified, the warrant authorizes a later review of the media or information consistent with the warrant. The time for executing the warrant in Rule 41(e)(2)(A) and (f)(1)(A) refers to the seizure or on-site copying of the media or information, and not to any later off-site copying or review.

(C) *Warrant for a Tracking Device.* A tracking-device warrant must identify the person or property to be tracked, designate the magistrate judge to whom it must be returned, and specify a reasonable length of time that the device may be used.

The time must not exceed 45 days from the date the warrant was issued. The court may, for good cause, grant one or more extensions for a reasonable period not to exceed 45 days each. The warrant must command the officer to:

    (i) complete any installation authorized by the warrant within a specified time no longer than 10 calendar days;

    (ii) perform any installation authorized by the warrant during the daytime, unless the judge for good cause expressly authorizes installation at another time; and

    (iii) return the warrant to the judge designated in the warrant.

(3) **Warrant by Telephonic or Other Means.** If a magistrate judge decides to proceed under Rule 41(d)(3)(A), the following additional procedures apply:

    (A) *Preparing a Proposed Duplicate Original Warrant.* The applicant must prepare a "proposed duplicate original warrant" and must read or otherwise transmit the contents of that document verbatim to the magistrate judge.

    (B) *Preparing an Original Warrant.* If the applicant reads the contents of the proposed duplicate original warrant, the magistrate judge must enter those contents into an original warrant. If the applicant transmits the contents by reliable electronic means, that transmission may serve as the original warrant.

    (C) *Modification.* The magistrate judge may modify the original warrant. The judge must transmit any modified warrant to the applicant by reliable electronic means under Rule 41(e)(3)(D) or direct the applicant to modify the proposed duplicate original warrant accordingly.

    (D) *Signing the Warrant.* Upon determining to issue the warrant, the magistrate judge must immediately sign the original warrant, enter on its face the exact date and time it is issued, and transmit it by reliable electronic means to the applicant or direct the applicant to sign the judge's name on the duplicate original warrant.

(f) **Executing and Returning the Warrant.**

(1) **Warrant to Search for and Seize a Person or Property.**

    (A) *Noting the Time.* The officer executing the warrant must enter on it the exact date and time it was executed.

(B) *Inventory.* An officer present during the execution of the warrant must prepare and verify an inventory of any property seized. The officer must do so in the presence of another officer and the person from whom, or from whose premises, the property was taken. If either one is not present, the officer must prepare and verify the inventory in the presence of at least one other credible person. In a case involving the seizure of electronic storage media or the seizure or copying of electronically stored information, the inventory may be limited to describing the physical storage media that were seized or copied. The officer may retain a copy of the electronically stored information that was seized or copied.

(C) *Receipt.* The officer executing the warrant must give a copy of the warrant and a receipt for the property taken to the person from whom, or from whose premises, the property was taken or leave a copy of the warrant and receipt at the place where the officer took the property. For a warrant to use remote access to search electronic storage media and seize or copy electronically stored information, the officer must make reasonable efforts to serve a copy of the warrant and receipt on the person whose property was searched or who possessed the information that was seized or copied. Service may be accomplished by any means, including electronic means, reasonably calculated to reach that person.

(D) *Return.* The officer executing the warrant must promptly return it—together with a copy of the inventory—to the magistrate judge designated on the warrant. The judge must, on request, give a copy of the inventory to the person from whom, or from whose premises, the property was taken and to the applicant for the warrant.

(2) Warrant for a Tracking Device.

(A) *Noting the Time.* The officer executing a tracking-device warrant must enter on it the exact date and time the device was installed and the period during which it was used.

(B) *Return.* Within 10 calendar days after the use of the tracking device has ended, the officer executing the warrant must return it to the judge designated in the warrant.

(C) *Service.* Within 10 calendar days after the use of the tracking device has ended, the officer executing a tracking-device warrant must serve a copy of the warrant on the person who was tracked or whose property was tracked. Service may be accomplished by delivering a copy to the person who, or whose property, was tracked; or by leaving a copy at the person's residence or usual place of abode with an individual of suitable age and discretion who resides at that location and by mailing a copy to the person's last known address. Upon request of the government, the judge may delay notice as provided in Rule 41(f)(3).

(3) Delayed Notice. Upon the government's request, a magistrate judge—or if authorized by Rule 41(b), a judge of a state court of record—may delay any notice required by this rule if the delay is authorized by statute.

(g) Motion to Return Property. A person aggrieved by an unlawful search and seizure of property or by the deprivation of property may move for the property's return. The motion must be filed in the district where the property was seized. The court must receive evidence on any factual issue necessary to decide the motion. If it grants the motion, the court must return the property to the movant, but may impose reasonable conditions to protect access to the property and its use in later proceedings.

(h) Motion to Suppress. A defendant may move to suppress evidence in the court where the trial will occur, as Rule 12 provides.

(i) Forwarding Papers to the Clerk. The magistrate judge to whom the warrant is returned must attach to the warrant a copy of the return, of the inventory, and of all other related papers and must deliver them to the clerk in the district where the property was seized.